# SMALL FISHY BITES

## Marisa Raniolo Wilkins

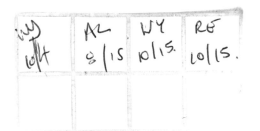

First published in 2013 by
New Holland Publishers
London • Sydney • Cape Town • Auckland

www.newhollandpublishers.com

Garfield House 86–88 Edgware Road London W2 2EA United Kingdom
Wembley Square First Floor Solan Road Gardens Cape Town 8001 South Africa
1/66 Gibbes Street Chatswood NSW 2067 Australia
218 Lake Road Northcote Auckland New Zealand

A catalogue record of this book is available at the British Library and at the National Library of Australia

ISBN: 9781742574394

10 9 8 7 6 5 4 3 2 1

Managing Director: Fiona Schultz
Publisher: Lliane Clarke
Editor: Jodi De Vantier
Designer: Tracy Loughlin
Stylist: Jodi Wuesterwald
Food photographer: Sue Stubbs
Production director: Olga Dementiev
Printer: Toppan Leefung Printing Ltd

Follow New Holland Publishers on
Facebook: www.facebook.com/NewHollandPublishers

# SMALL FISHY BITES

NEW
HOLLAND

## Marisa Raniolo Wilkins

To all my friends who enjoy eating and cooking fish and whose contributions have enlarged my repertoire of recipes.

## Acknowledgements

*Le idee migliori sono proprietà di tutti.*
*The best ideas are common property.*
Lucio Anneo Seneca
Roman philosopher, playwright, politician and writer (5 BC – 65AD).

I would like to thank my friends who generously contributed recipes to *Small Fishy Bites*, which will now become common property.

When I write I make little time to do anything else. I would therefore also like to thank all those I have neglected during the time I spent researching and writing this book, particularly my friends and family, and my partner, who has been closest to the project and probably endured the worst of my temperaments.

This is the second book I've had published by New Holland. I'm grateful to Lliane Clarke for asking me to write it and having faith that I'd complete it.

# Contents

# Introduction

I love eating fish. Saltwater, fresh water, scales or shells—I love eating all kinds of fish and seafood, cooked and raw, skinless fillets or with fins and bones or tentacles. I love it smoked, salted and pickled.

My taste for fish goes back to my childhood, split between two cultures— the north and south of Italy—stretching from Trieste to Sicily.

Trieste hugs the Istrian coast at the tip of the Adriatic, blending its Austro-Hungarian influences with the neighbouring cultures of Slovenia and Croatia. While, deep in the south, Sicily basks in swells of the Mediterranean. An arrow-headed island whose culture is the sum of countless conquests by Greeks, Carthaginians, Romans, Moors, Normans, Spaniards and the French.

In Trieste, I would go shopping for fish at the market with my mother. I watched the fish vendor chopping up eels, which would still be wriggling as we carried them home. When we bought mussels he would pour scoops of sea water into the package to keep them fresh.

Sicily was for summer holidays with my grandparents and relatives. In the markets I'd see huge carcasses of tuna and swordfish and displays of other fish I'd never seen in Trieste. I also collected sea urchins underneath rocks on the beach and ate them raw and watched fishermen beating octopus on the rocks to tenderise them.

When my parents migrated, we discovered that fish was not eaten as often as we were used to in Italy. My friends ate fish and chips once a week on Friday nights and it came wrapped in newspaper from the fish and chips shop. What was interesting to us was that there were many settlers from Greece who ran these businesses.

In those days, fish was also sometimes served as a starter, perhaps as a shrimp cocktail appetiser at a restaurant or prepared at home when there were invited guests or at a party when cocktail shrimp appeared on buttered bread or at the end of toothpicks with a decorative onion.

The more some things change, the more some other things don't. Even now I have found that often some hosts may prefer to offer a fishy bite as a starter—an appetiser—rather than cook fish as a main meal. Consequently, there is a sense of celebration associated with eating fish.

## In praise of presenting fishy bites

*Small Fishy Bites* celebrates the diversity and versatility of seafood. These recipes recognise the popularity of serving small helpings—easy, casual and varied dishes.

Small morsels are convivial fare that can be shared at social gatherings—picnics, parties, get togethers. On other occasions, small bites provide an accompaniment to drinks.

Easily managed, bite-sized pieces that once were known as nibbles, finger food or canapés have morphed into spuntini, tapas, dim sum or mezze, reflecting the widening repertoire of cuisines we are exposed to, especially the Asian and Mediterranean flavours.

There are different ways to appreciate the cultures of different countries and one of these is through their cuisine. Mealtimes are an important part of daily life. Eating and sharing food with others is at least as much about socialising as sustenance.

In many cultures small courses are designed to stimulate the appetite not satisfy hunger. The French hors d'oeuvre, literally means outside of work, a snack outside of work hours.

Small plates of savouries are very common in some cultures, for example, in Spain where the idea of tapas provides a way for diners to enjoy casual eating and to sample multiple, intriguing tastes, in a single meal. Tapas are so entrenched in Spain and in other countries where Spaniards have settled that they make a distinction between the various types of fingerfood and appetisers that are served at the bar. They have *Cosas de Picar* (pick with fingers), *Pinchos* or *Pintxos* (eat with a toothpick or skewer) and *Caszuelas* (usually in a sauce and needs greater care in eating and therefore served in a bowl).

In some cultures, notably Arabic cultures, an array of small dishes can be the entire meal. The Scandinavians have passed on to the rest of us the appreciation of smorgasbord.

Small plates are an easy and pleasant way to sample a range flavours without the commitment to one entrée or the different courses. And what a pleasant way to socialise!

## As a cook

I do not claim to be an expert in any of the cuisines that I have written about in the book. They are the results of my experiments and variations with ingredients and flavours in my kitchen. For me, cooking is an adventure and I am influenced by what I have eaten, what I've read about, what new ingredients I encounter and environmental issues I'm aware of.

I'm excited when I find new produce at the market, which often inspires a new recipe or prompts me to apply what I know about a similar ingredient and cook it in a similar way. You may find this is obvious when you see how I have applied what I know generally about flavours and combinations of particular cuisines to recipes from particular cultures. For example, you are likely to find saffron and pimenton in the Spanish-style recipes or a concentration on shredded ginger in Asian-influenced recipes. And, I am probably making the same gaffe (the Italian word for a faux pas) when I experiment with the cooking of other cultures as non-Italians do when they add dried tomatoes and bocconcini to any dish that is supposed to be Italian.

In the last few years and with the ever-evolving food culture where I live, there has been a growing interest in Latin American treats: papusas, arepas, a variety of Chilean breads, tortillas and empanadas. I realise this reveals a gap in my knowledge and experience of the cuisine of Latin American countries. I have not visited any of these countries, but I wanted to include some of these recipes in the book because of their growing popularity.

Home cooks are using their experiences to create and recreate recipes, to embellish and reproduce recipes. As cooks, we have become cross-cultural. Interest in other cuisines through travel or vicarious experiences by reading recipes, watching TV cooking shows and exposure to a greater range of ingredients have whetted our appetites and enlarged our repertoires.

Cooks are willing to replicate foods they may have eaten in a market or street stall, a bar or an eatery, or try new recipes or adapt them to suit personal tastes.

For example, salmon or tuna patties were once made with tinned fish, onions and mashed potatoes. In our present culture we may still enjoy making and eating these, but now we may be more likely to be making fish cakes with fresh fish and dip them into a spicy Thai sauce or present them with a dill mayonnaise.

It should also come as no surprise that a dish, which is a speciality of one cuisine, has its equivalents in other cultures. For example, there is more than one way to enjoy fried squid: *calamari fritti* (Italian: squid, lightly dipped in flour and fried, presented with fresh lemon), salt and pepper squid (Asian: squid dipped in batter and dipped in a spicy mixture which includes salt and pepper) or squid coated in a saffron batter and served with aioli. All good, each similar but different, and an indication how our cooking has been influenced by what we experience.

Although I have written a book about cooking fish (*Sicilian Seafood Cooking*) my cooking isn't confined to just Italian or Sicilian food. But you will find that many of the recipes in *Small Fishy Bites* have an Italian base or use Italian ingredients.

For example, I tend to use extra virgin oil for everything; I am not a great fan of processed food; and I like to make everything myself. So, yes—I do make my own egg mayonnaise and pastry. But that doesn't mean that you have to. It is your choice and there are readymade ingredients in stores and supermarkets.

I always buy salted capers rather than those pickled in vinegar because I find the vinegar dominates the flavour of the capers and it's the capers I want to taste—not the vinegar. And for that pleasure I'm prepared to spend the short time it takes to rinse the salted capers, let them soak for a little longer, and then rinse them again before I use them.

I always use what some call 'sea salt' and, as a true Italian, I cook dishes when the ingredients are in the season, because that is when they taste the best.

## About fish

I know that for some people cooking at home, whole fish with bones and scales are a challenge. Many people prefer to buy and eat boneless fish fillets with a medium to firm texture. It is a convenient and easy option. To that preference, I would only add that, whenever possible, I buy fish that is caught or grown using sustainable fishing practices that do not threaten the existing stocks of a particular fish or harm the environment. What is sustainable in one location may not be in another and finding out whether a particular fish is sustainable or not may take a great deal of effort.

When I spoke to different people about the fish they preferred to cook and eat, salmon and shrimp/prawns seem to be the most common and most appreciated. I was pleasantly surprised to learn at an Aquaculture Conference that the environmental practices across the aquaculture industry have significantly improved and that there is legislation in many countries that ensures that the highest international standards of responsible aquaculture are further developed and maintained.

I understand that wild fisheries cannot catch all of the fish we eat, but minimising the environmental impact of the way fish are harvested or farmed is really important to me. So, I tend to buy flathead, sardines, bream, snapper, whiting and gurnard, and avoid blue-fin tuna, orange roughie, marlin and swordfish (which is, sadly, the prized favourite of Sicilians).

If you are interested in sourcing sustainable fish species ask your fish vendor and consult the internet. A good fish vendor will answer your questions, sell a variety of fish and be willing to assist and to recommend particular fish types for various recipes.

The flavour of fish varies from mild to strong, and usually the darker the flesh, the oilier the fish and the stronger the taste. White-fleshed fish are mild tasting; cream-fleshed fish are moderately flavourful; and dark-fleshed fish are intensely flavourful.

I think fish tastes better when it's cooked with the skin and bones still attached, but in *Small Fishy Bites*, the focus is on making sprightly snacks that are easy and quick to prepare, so fish fillets are convenient. That is also why there are lots of recipes for smoked fish. So many varieties of fish taste great when smoked—salmon, mackerel, trout and eel to name the most popular. They are versatile, long lasting, ready to eat and ideal for catering whether it is dinners, buffets or holiday celebrations.

Shrimp/prawns and squid also are boneless and a favourite with guests. They are also convenient and easy to prepare. Oysters, mussels, cockles and scallops are the show-off foods and unless guests have an allergy to shellfish you cannot go wrong serving them.

## How I compiled the recipes

As part of my preparation for writing *Small Fishy Bites*, I decided to ask around to see what morsels and treats friends and acquaintances were preparing. Some are avid travellers and good cooks who love entertaining and sharing food with others. All the friends I consulted said that they prefer to prepare the makings of a recipe beforehand so that as hosts they can socialise with their guests and, therefore, *Small Fishy Bites* is also about taking short cuts. These recipes are meant to be easy. Some are so simple I debated whether I should include them.

The way fishy bites are presented can be a lot of fun and the possibilities are boundless. There can be toothpicks/ sticks/skewers, in spoons, coffee cups and shot glasses, on so many bases—pastry, canapés, bread, crisp breads, fried polenta, corn bread, buckwheat blinis—or topped with pastry. Small individual serves or presented in large platters do not require much imagination, but food could also be presented in bento boxes, wrapped in paper, bread or leaves. I have made spreads and dips and put them into small preserving jars, or used old-style ramekins and mini-casseroles.

So *avanti*: go forward with it and enjoy cooking and eating fishy bites.

# Tidbits

*Braised calamari can be made days before and it stores well in the fridge. It is a common recipe throughout Italy (a tegame is a shallow sauté pan with a lid). Cooking squid can be tricky. There is a fine line between tender and rubbery. It can be cooked on high heat for a short time (in no more than 5–8 minutes) or a long time on slow heat (for at least 30–40 minutes). When you cook squid for a short time, it may still look a little shiny, but the residual heat completes the job and the flesh will turn opaque. If you cook the squid for longer, the juices will have more taste. This recipe is the easy option.*

# Sautéed squid with peas and potatoes

## Calamari in tegame
### Serves 6–8

36oz/1kg small squid

2 tablespoons extra virgin olive oil

1 onion, chopped

¼ cup white wine

1 cup shelled, cooked peas

3–4 cooked potatoes (use less or more according to personal tastes)

½ cup flat leaf parsley, cut finely

salt and freshly ground pepper to taste

**TOMATO SALSA**

6 fresh, ripe tomatoes, peeled and chopped or a can (with the liquid)

extra virgin olive oil

garlic cloves, left whole

fresh basil or oregano

salt and pepper, to taste

To make the salsa, place all of the ingredients into a pan together and cook until the sauce has thickened.

If you are cleaning the squid yourself, prepare the squid by removing the head with a sharp knife. Open the body and remove the internal organs.

Wipe clean or wash the squid and cut into strips.

Heat the oil in a frying pan and sauté the peeled, chopped onions lightly.

Add the squid and sauté for about 5–7 minutes. Remove the squid, pour in the white wine and evaporate a little on a medium–high heat.

Add the squid, tomato salsa, peas, potatoes and parsley.

Cover and cook gently for about 5 minutes depending on how well you like your squid cooked. Season to taste.

*Cooking fish in a pouch made from baking parchment/paper that is folded and sealed is called* en papilliote, *which comes from the French word for butterfly. Fish can be cooked in foil just as well, but I usually line the foil with a piece of baking parchment/paper, spread some oil or butter on it and place the fish directly onto it. You can use any small-sized fish as single serves for each of your guests, but for convenience sake, you may wish to use fillets or pieces of boned fish, about 3 in/8 cm. The packages are very easy to handle, save kitchen mess and look fabulous. Just warn your guests when they open the parcels to be careful of the steam.*

# Fish in a parcel

## Fish en papilliote

any small-sized fish or pieces of boned fish (one parcel for each guest) • extra virgin olive oil or butter • salt and pepper, to taste • lemon juice, to taste • lemon or lime wedges, to serve

COMBINATIONS • chopped scallions/spring onions and a slice of pancetta • a red cherry tomato, some black or green olives and either basil or oregano • a few crushed fennel seeds, a little chopped parsley and a thin slice of lemon • tarragon and capers, and butter instead of oil • garlic, parsley and oregano • anchovies, rosemary and a thin slice of lemon • bay leaf, rosemary or thyme and grated lemon peel • chopped anchovies, mint and a few pine nuts • a few slices of thinly sliced chorizo, chopped scallions/spring onions and a pinch of pimenton (Spanish paprika) • preserved lemons, ground cumin, fresh cilantro/coriander and fresh mint
ASIAN COMBINATION • kaffir lime leaves • a stalk of lemon grass • coriander or Thai basil • garlic or chilli • grated ginger • coconut cream or green or red curry paste
MIDDLE EASTERN COMBINATION • dried coriander, cumin, cinnamon, garlic or chilli • pomegranate molasses or tahini

Cut foil into squares about 7¾ x 7¾ in (20 x 20 cm). Place a smaller piece of baking parchment/paper in the centre, about 4 ¾ x 4 ¾ in (12 x 12 cm).

Smear the baking parchment/paper with a little extra virgin olive oil or butter. Place the fish on top of this. To each parcel, add a combination (as listed above) of herbs and spices of your choice and a little more oil or butter and a squeeze of lemon or lime juice. Take each end of the packet (the side nearest you and the side farthest from you) and fold it over tightly in the centre of the parcel. Leave a little space for steam around the fish, and roll the sides tightly until they feel secure enough to stay closed.

To cook, preheat the oven to 430°F/220°C. Place the fish parcels on a baking tray and cook them for about 4–5 minutes. Rest the fish out of the oven for 5–10 minutes. The fish will keep on cooking so by the time you present it to your guests it will be ready to eat. If you are cooking the parcels of fish on a barbecue, cook on a moderately high heat.

*This is a very simple frittata. You can replace the shrimp/prawns with 9 oz/250 g of white crabmeat, if you prefer. Make sure you drain it well. You can also use mussel meat. I cook my frittata as the Italians do — in a frying pan and never set in the oven. After all, a frittata means something that is fried. The frittata I make is about ½in/1.5cm thick. A tomato salad goes well with this frittata.*

# Shrimp frittata with a simple tomato salad

### Serves 6–8

9 oz/250 g green, shelled shrimp/
    prawns or crabmeat
8–10 eggs
salt and freshly ground pepper
    to taste
¼ cup of extra virgin olive oil
    plus 2 oz/50 g unsalted butter,
    for frying
2 scallions/spring onions, finely
    sliced
1 tablespoon of parsley, finely
    chopped

**SIMPLE TOMATO SALAD**

4 large tomatoes, sliced
2 scallions/spring onions, thinly
    sliced
salt and pepper, to taste
2 tablespoons extra virgin
    olive oil
fresh basil leaves, to serve

Slice the shrimp in half.

Beat the eggs slightly with a fork, add a pinch of salt and pepper.

Heat the oil and butter, and sauté the spring onions with the prawns until they change colour. Add the parsley and soften.

Pour the eggs into a medium-sized frying pan and, as the frittata sets, lift the sides to help it cook more quickly. Press the top of the frittata down with the spatula.

Turn the frittata out onto a plate, and then slide it back upside down into the frying pan to cook the other side. You may need to use a little more oil and butter in the frying pan.

To make the tomato salad, place the sliced tomatoes in one layer on a platter.

Top with the thinly sliced scallions. Season to taste and drizzle with the olive oil. Scatter with the fresh basil leaves and serve with the frittata.

The frittata can be eaten hot or cold. The combination tastes even better if eaten with good quality, fresh crusty bread.

*Char-grilled octopus is popular all over the Mediterranean. Rosemary is a herb usually associated with the cooking of meat; however as a variation, try it instead of the oregano. It is quite usual to blanch the octopus before grilling it.*

# Char-grilled octopus

## Serves 6–8

Place the octopus into a saucepan with 2 tablespoons of water and a pinch of salt.

Cover and cook over low-medium heat for 10 minutes, or until the octopus changes colour and curls up. Remove from heat and allow to cool.

Combine all the marinade ingredients in a large bowl.

Cut the octopus into manageable pieces. Clean any offending bits (I always leave the suckers and the pink skin on but many cooks remove these). Place in the marinade and turn to coat.

Cover and refrigerate for at least 1–2 hours (the octopus will not spoil if left for longer). Drain the octopus well before grilling.

Place the octopus on a hot barbecue and cook for 4 to 5 minutes per side. Brush with marinade as it cooks.

Serve the leftover marinade as a sauce. However, if you feel squeamish about this, place the marinade into a small saucepan and bring it to the boil. Add some more extra virgin olive oil and a little more lemon juice and, if you wish, a little finely chopped parsley.

70 oz/2 kg octopus (tentacles)

SIMPLE MARINADE
½ cup extra-virgin olive oil plus extra to serve
1 teaspoon chilli flakes or freshly ground black pepper
juice of 1 lemon plus extra to serve
2 garlic cloves, finely chopped
salt to taste
1 teaspoon dried oregano
parsely, finely chopped, to garnish

*I have always used marinades before grilling any fish. If I am presenting the fish with a sauce, I keep the marinade simple so it doesn't compete with the flavours. For these grilled shrimp/prawns I use a garnish of fried breadcrumbs as the finishing condiment. My standard marinade acts as a vehicle to lubricate the prawns. Guests will easily eat three shrimp/prawns each. Estimate how many shrimp/prawns you need using the following amounts as a guide. They cook very quickly, so watch them carefully as they cook.*

# Italian grilled shrimp with a fried breadcrumb and herb garnish

### Serves 6

24 green shrimp/prawns, shells on

## MARINADE

½ cup extra virgin olive oil
2 cloves minced garlic
3 tablespoons lemon juice
freshly ground black pepper or
    chilli flakes
2–3 fresh bay leaves

## MUDDICA ATTURRATA

1 cup fresh breadcrumbs (made
    with 1–3-day-old bread)
2 tablespoons extra virgin olive oil
1 teaspoon sugar
½ cup pine nuts, toasted
½ cup finely chopped parsley
2 cloves garlic, minced
zest of 1 lemon
salt and freshly ground pepper
1–2 anchovies (optional)
½ teaspoon nutmeg (optional)

## GREMOLATA

½ cup parsley, finely chopped
2 cloves garlic, minced
zest of 2 lemons and juice of 1
¼ cup extra virgin olive oil

Mix the ingredients for the marinade together. Add the shrimp, tossing them to coat. Leave these to marinate at least three hours in the refrigerator. Continue to move them around during the time that they are marinating.

Grill prawns on a hot grill plate for about five minutes, turning once or alternatively, cook them in a frying pan over high heat.

Arrange the prawns on a large serving platter and scatter with one of the following combinations.

## MUDDICA ATTURRATA (SICILIAN-STYLE GARNISH)
*Fried breadcrumbs are used frequently in Sicilian cooking. This is the mixture that I often use as a stuffing—the nutmeg and anchovies are optional.*

In a non-stick frying pan, toast the breadcrumbs over a low flame in 1 tablespoon of the olive oil, until golden. Remove from the heat and add the sugar, mix well and then add the remaining oil, stirring it in gently. Set aside to cool.

Stir in all of the other ingredients.

## GREMOLATA (MILANESE-STYLE GARNISH)
*If you've cooked osso bucco, you'll know about sprinkling the meat with a combination of parsley, garlic and lemon zest. When I am using gremolata over fish I also add extra ingredients.*

Mix all of the ingredients together.

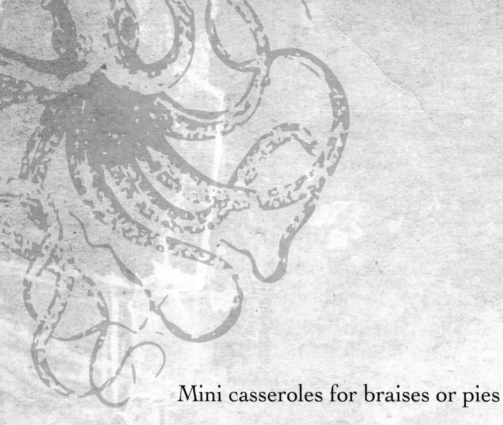

# Mini casseroles for braises or pies

As a present, a friend gave me some colourful, enamelled, cast-iron mini 'casseroles' or 'Dutch ovens' and I love them. They are brought to the table straight from the oven so tell your guests to be ultra careful when they eat from them. Also, protect your table with mats.

I make mini-braises to eat with bread or I cover the dishes with puff or shortcrust pastry or with mashed potatoes, like mini-potpies. They can also be baked in pie tins.

Braising is cooking in a small amount of liquid. You can use wines, fruit juices and pulps (especially tomato pulp or lemon juice) or leftover juices from other fish cooking or fish stock (including the liquid released from steaming mussels or cockles—this can be salty so decrease the salt used). Unlike meats, which are braised long and slow, fish is braised only long enough to cook it through. Different herbs and spices will also vary the taste of the final dish.

Make the pastry yourself, or just buy readymade puff or shortcrust pastry (thawed if frozen). If you plan to cover your fish braise with pastry use a cold filling before covering with pastry.

Place the mini casseroles on a baking sheet/tray (to prevent any spillage from making a mess at the bottom of your oven). Select fish of a size that will fit into your mini casserole dishes.

Here are four very different combinations to play with, and you can vary ingredients to suit your tastes.

*This is a more delicate version and can be made with skinless, boned fillets of white fish or salmon. You could also include shrimp or scallops. Thick cream, butter or egg yolks can be used to thicken the sauce. If you would like a topping, creamy mashed potato is perfect with this.*

# A refined braise with French or English flavours

## Serves 6

Preheat the oven to 430°F/220°C.

Melt 1 tablespoon of butter and the oil in a frying pan and over low-medium heat soften the onion with some seasoning until soft and translucent.

Add the herbs halfway through the cooking.

Remove the contents from the pan and cool.

Heat a little more butter in the same frying pan and lightly fry the fish pieces (sprinkled with a little salt) on both sides, turning once only. Remove from the pan and cool.

Boil the diced potato in a saucepan until soft. Mash with the butter and milk and season with salt and pepper. Set aside, covered.

There should be some residual juices in the pan. To this, add the wine first and evaporate slightly before you add the stock.

Whisk in the butter or cream.

Cook slowly, without boiling, until the sauce thickens. Return the fish pieces to the sauce.

Spoon into each mini-casserole some of the onion mixture. Place 1 piece of fish and some of the sauce in each.

Cover with buttery mashed potato, topped with dots of extra butter.

Bake for 7–10 minutes. You may need to cover the mashed potato with a small piece of foil if the potato looks as if it will brown too quickly.

1 tablespoon extra virgin olive oil plus 1 tablespoon butter to cook the fish

1 small onion or 2 scallions/ spring onions, chopped

salt, pepper to taste

fresh herbs, use one or more: tarragon, parsley, dill, chervil, bay leaves

6 pieces of salmon fillets or white fish, cut into bite-sized pieces or use a mixture of fish and shellfish

24 oz/700 g potatoes, peeled and diced

2 tablespoons butter plus extra

a little milk

salt and freshly ground pepper

1 cup white wine

1 cup fish stock

2 tablespoons unsalted butter or thick cream, to thicken

# A braise with olives and Mediterranean flavours

*Serves 6*

Preheat the oven to 430°F/220°C.

Heat the extra virgin olive oil in a frying pan and pan-fry the fish lightly. Add a little salt. Remove the fish and set aside.

Add the other ingredients and sauté, until the juice of the tomatoes is reduced.

Spoon some of the tomato mixture into each mini-casserole. Place 1 piece of fish in each and top with more tomato.

Either cover with a lid (or metal foil) and bake.

If you wish to cover the casseroles with pastry, cool your ingredients beforehand and then place a circle of short or puff pastry on top of the braise (cut slightly larger than the mini casserole). Dampen the edges of the mini casserole to seal the pastry.

Place an extra strip of pastry around the edges and decorate the edges with a pastry wheel or fork (optional).

Brush pastry with oil or butter or a beaten egg yolk mixed with a little water. This will give the pastry colour and shine.

Place the mini casseroles on a baking sheet/tray and cook until the pastry is golden. Serve hot.

2 tablespoons extra virgin olive oil

6 pieces of fish (1 serve per person)

salt, pepper or chilli flakes to taste

12 green olives or black olives, stoned and sliced

4 large red tomatoes, peeled and chopped

1 tablespoon capers

1–2 cloves garlic, chopped finely

herbs, use one or more: fresh parsley, oregano, fennel or basil, chopped, to taste

oil or butter, or a beaten egg yolk mixed with a little water, to brush pastry

*I love this combination inspired by a favourite old Moroccan recipe of Paula Wolfert. She stuffs a whole fish with a paste of blanched almonds, orange flower water, cinnamon, icing sugar and butter. The fish is then cooked with onions and saffron. Here is my version.*

# Baked white fish with almond paste

## Serves 6

6 pieces white fish, cut into bite-sized pieces or left whole

2 onions or 4 scallions/spring onions, finely sliced

2 tablespoons extra virgin olive oil

1–2 pinches of saffron (soaked in a little warm water)

salt, pepper to taste

### PASTE

9 oz/250 g blanched almonds

1 tablespoon extra virgin olive oil

3 tablespoons butter, softened

2 teaspoons orange flower water

1 teaspoon cinnamon

1 teaspoon confectioner's/icing sugar

2-3 tablespoons water

Preheat the oven to 400°F/200°C.

To make the paste, toast the blanched almonds in oil, then pulverise in a food processor.

Add the butter, orange flower water, cinnamon, confectioner's sugar and mix in the water until you have a smooth paste.

In a frying pan and over low-medium heat, soften the onion with some oil with seasoning until translucent. Remove from the pan and cool.

Heat the rest of the oil in the same frying pan and lightly fry the fish pieces (sprinkled with a little salt) on both sides, turning once only. Add saffron water. Remove from the pan and cool.

Distribute onions in each mini casserole. Top each with about 1 tablespoon of the paste—flatten this with your palms into a thin layer. Add fish and any juices. Top with remaining paste (also flattened). Cover with a lid and bake in the oven for 7–10 minutes.

*An old Greek favourite and the combination of tomatoes, shrimp and feta is irresistible. Mop up this braise with crusty bread.*

# Baked shrimp and feta
## Shrimp saganaki
### Serves 6

Preheat the oven to 430°F/220°C.

Gently fry the onion in half the oil until translucent.

Add garlic, tomatoes (if canned use some of the juice), wine, herbs and seasoning. Cover and simmer gently until thickened.

Heat the rest of the oil in a frying pan and sauté the shrimp lightly (about 1 minute). Add a little salt.

Distribute prawns into the mini casseroles and spoon in the tomato sauce.

Coarsely crumble feta cheese into largish chunks and sprinkle on top; push the cheese slightly below the surface. Cook in the very hot oven for 6–10 minutes until the feta has melted and lightly browned.

Sprinkle with parsley and serve immediately.

1 onion or 3 scallions/spring onions, finely chopped

3 tablespoons extra virgin olive oil

2-3 cloves garlic, finely chopped

4-5 large, peeled, red tomatoes or use 1 x 14–14¾oz/ 400–425g can

½ cup dry white wine

½ teaspoon dried oregano and fresh basil, to taste

salt and freshly ground pepper

5-6 green shrimps/prawns per mini casserole, shelled, tails left on

5½ oz/160 g feta cheese

1 tablespoon fresh parsley, finely chopped to decorate

*These shrimp/prawns can be presented on a platter and guests can use toothpicks or small forks to skewer them. They are sufficiently spicy not to require a dipping sauce but, if you would like to add one, what can be fun (and is an easy option) is to give your guests a dipping bowl so that they can mix their own sauces. On the table place small containers of soy sauce, vinegar (Chinese vinegar if you wish), chilli oil and crushed garlic. Estimate how many shrimp/prawns you need using the following amounts as a guide.*

# Shrimp with Asian Flavours

## Serves 6

24 large green shrimp/prawns cleaned, heads removed, shelled and butterflied to remove the vein with the waste.

MARINADE
1–2 fresh, red chillies, thinly sliced, according to taste
1 tablespoon grated ginger
1 tablespoon minced garlic
1 tablespoon vegetable oil
1 tablespoon lime juice and zest
1 tablespoon soy sauce
Kaffir lime leaves, optional

First, prepare the marinade. Remove the seeds from the chilli and chop into small pieces or strips.

Combine the chilli and the rest of the marinade ingredients. If you have some Kaffir lime leaves pop them into the marinade as well.

Marinate the prawns in this mixture for at least 1 hour.

Place the prawns on a hot grill plate on a barbecue. They will only take 2–3 minutes to cook. Turn them only once.

*These little morsels are fish fillets rolled around a light stuffing—only herbs and garlic are used. Fillets of small fish (with skin on) are suitable: anything from mild-flavoured whiting, stronger-tasting flathead to even stronger, oilier fish such as mullet or sardines. You can use dry Marsala wine or Manzanilla sherry to caramelise the juices and make a delicious coating for the rolled fish. An alternative is to use orange juice (juice of 2 oranges) instead of the Marsala and use fresh basil for the stuffing.*

# Fish fillets rolled around a herb stuffing

## Involtini di pesce
### Serves 6

6 fish fillets from small fish
salt and freshly ground pepper
use one or more of any fresh
    herbs: rosemary, parsley,
    marjoram and oregano
2 cloves garlic, finely chopped
grated peel of 1 orange or lemon
¼ cup extra virgin olive oil
fresh bay leaves
½ cup dry Marsala wine

Flatten each fillet if necessary; if using large fillets, cut into smaller strips. Sprinkle each with a little salt and pepper.

Mix the herbs, garlic and peel with 1 tablespoon of the olive oil. Place a little of the stuffing at one end of each fillet and roll up. Secure each roll with a toothpick.

Sauté fish rolls in remaining extra virgin olive oil.

Add bay leaves and continue to cook the fish until it is almost ready.

Remove the fish from the pan and set aside (it will keep on cooking with the residual heat).

Add Marsala to caramelise the juices and reduce the sauce—this will take only take a few minutes.

Return the fish rolls to the pan to heat and to coat in the sauce.

Remove bay leaves and serve.

*This recipe was used in my book* Sicilian Seafood Cooking *and I am reproducing it here because these are scrumptious. And I wouldn't change a thing in the recipe. There are local variations in the ingredients used for the stuffing, the method of cooking and for the names of the dish in other parts of Sicily. These are my favourite ingredients for this recipe from a combination of local recipes.*

# Rolled stuffed sardines

## Sarde a beccafico

### Serves 6

12 fillets of fresh sardines

½ cup breadcrumbs made with good quality 1–2-day-old bread

¼ extra virgin olive oil

¼ cup pine nuts

¼ cup currants

¼ cup parsley, cut finely

4 finely anchovy fillets, cut finely

juice and zest of 1 lemon

¼ teaspoon nutmeg

salt and freshly ground pepper to taste

2 cloves garlic, chopped

12 bay leaves, fresh

1 teaspoon sugar

Scale, gut, butterfly and clean sardines and leave the tail. If you buy fillets, they are sold without tails—this doesn't matter, but when the fillet of the sardine is closed around the stuffing, the tail is flicked upright to resemble a bird, so this may be missing.

Wipe each sardine dry before stuffing.

Preheat oven to 400°F/200°C.

To prepare the stuffing, toast breadcrumbs until golden in about 1 tablespoon of the extra virgin olive oil (I use a non-stick frying pan) over a low flame. Take off the heat and cool.

Stir in pine nuts, currants, parsley, anchovies, lemon zest, nutmeg, salt, pepper and garlic.

Add a little more extra virgin olive oil if the mixture is dry.

Place a spoonful of the stuffing in each opened sardine and close it upon itself to resemble a fat bird (any leftover stuffing can be sprinkled on top to seal the fish). If using a fillet place a little of the stuffing at one end of each fillet and roll up. Secure each roll with a toothpick.

Position each sardine closely side by side in an oiled baking dish with tail sticking up and place a bay leaf between each fish.

Sprinkle the sardines with lemon juice and any leftover stuffing, the sugar and more oil.

Bake for 20–25 minutes.

*Although salmon is an oily fish it does not have an overpowering fishy taste and this may be why it is an extremely popular fish. It goes well with a vanilla-infused mayonnaise. As with all recipes, you can substitute one fish for another; any cutlet of firm white fish would be suitable. I particularly like wild barramundi. You can eat this hot or cold. A more robust sauce can be made with capers and anchovies (salsa di chiappareddi in Sicilian) and I particularly like this sauce as a contrast to the delicate tasting fish.*

# Salmon with vanilla mayonnaise on a caper sauce

## Serves 6

Preheat the oven to 430°F/220°C.

Dry the fish on paper towels and season the salmon fillets with a little salt and pepper on both sides.

Drizzle with a little olive oil and roast in the oven, skin side down for around 6–8 minutes.

Check to see if it is cooked to your liking. The flakes should separate without much resistance even if some parts still look translucent.

Cook the salmon for less time if you prefer it only seared on the outside and pinker.

Alternatively, pan-fry the salmon.

To make the vanilla mayonnaise, cut the vanilla bean in half lengthwise and scrape the seeds from the inside the vanilla bean. You can also cheat by using a little commercially made vanilla paste made from pure vanilla. Mix it well.

Add it to the mayonnaise (see recipe page 91) and the cream.

To make the caper sauce, heat the olive oil before adding the anchovies. These will dissolve in the oil. Take the pan off the heat. Add the minced garlic, parsley, capers and the vinegar or the juice of a lemon.

Cook for no longer than a minute. Be careful when you add the wet ingredients as the oil may splash.

6 pieces of salmon with skin on, thickly cut and about 1–4 in/8–10 cm long
salt and freshly ground black pepper
extra virgin olive oil

### VANILLA MAYONNAISE

1 vanilla bean
1 cup Mayonnaise (see recipe page 91)
1 tablespoon thick or sour cream

### CAPER SAUCE

2 tablespoons extra virgin olive oil
2 anchovies, cut into pieces
1 clove minced garlic
½ cup parsley, finely chopped (dried on paper towels beforehand)
3 tablespoons capers
1 tablespoon wine vinegar or the juice of 1 lemon

BOQUES
GALLEGUES / BOCA
GALLEGA
18

LLAGOSTÍ LANGOSTINO
10

CALAMARSSÒ / CHIPIRÓN
8

*These little rolls look wonderful and taste as good as they look. The friend who sent me this recipe loves smoked salmon and I have never been to her house without finding some in her fridge. She has a ready supply for herself and any of her welcome guests. Use baby asparagus or trim the stems of larger asparagus to a size that will fit the centre of each slice of smoked salmon. My friend suggests presenting these cigars/rolls garnished with watercress sprigs or purple basil shoots. Chives and the purple flowers of chives will also look sensational.*

# Smoked Salmon cigars with mayonnaise

## *Makes 12*

Mix together the mayonnaise, Dijon mustard and lemon juice with the finely flaked Atlantic smoked salmon or cooked fish to make a filling. When combined, add chives and green peppercorns. Mix well.

Lay one asparagus spear on top of a smoked salmon slice. Top with some filling, then roll to make a cigar shape. Repeat with the remaining asparagus spears and salmon slices.

2 tablespoons Mayonnaise (see recipe page 91)

2 teaspoons Dijon mustard

2 tablespoons lemon juice

6–7 oz/170–200 g smoked Atlantic salmon, finely flaked, or use cooked salmon

1 tablespoon chives, finely sliced

1 tablespoon soft green peppercorns, drained

12 asparagus spears, cooked

12 large slices smoked salmon (each slice needs to be large enough to hold the stuffing)

*This is quick, easy finger food to serve with drinks. Fresh lemon myrtle imparts a very aromatic taste to the ingredients, but it can be omitted. The other fresh herbs also provide a nice balance to the smoky oiliness of the salmon, the salty capers and the cream.*

# smoked salmon rolls

## Makes 12

Wash the herbs and dry between two layers of paper towel. Very finely shred the lemon myrtle leaves, if you're using them.

In a bowl, combine the mascarpone and lemon rind. Add some freshly cracked pepper.

Spoon some mascarpone onto one end of a small slice of smoked salmon.

Place several capers on the mascarpone and a few shreds of lemon myrtle leaf (or the dried version).

Lay a generous sprig of dill or fennel crosswise on the mascarpone so that when you roll the salmon the herb pokes out at one end.

Roll the salmon to enclose the filling. Place the rolls on a serving plate.

At this stage they can be covered and refrigerated until required.

Before serving, drizzle with good extra virgin olive oil and crack some black pepper over them.

handful of fresh fronds of dill, tarragon or fennel
4 young lemon myrtle leaves (optional)
7 oz/200 g mascarpone
finely grated rind of 1 lemon
cracked black pepper
12 slices of smoked salmon (each slice needs to be large enough to hold the stuffing)
3 tablespoon capers (salted taste best)
extra virgin olive oil
extra black pepper

*This recipe has been provided by a friend who catches all of her fish. Squid is easy to fish and when I go out on her boat I catch some too using a simple jag. They can be fried in a little extra virgin olive oil and a little butter and they can also be grilled. These also taste good cold and can be prepared beforehand. Refrigerate until needed and slice into bite-sized pieces. Squid vary in size and it is difficult to provide exact quantities for the stuffing — you may need a little more or less than is listed here.*

# squid bites

### Serves 6

1 good quality chorizo
½ cup red wine (optional)
7 oz/200 g feta
6 small squid tubes (body size approx. 5½in/14 cm in length)
extra virgin olive oil and a little butter, to fry

Cook the chorizo first, slice it, fry it and then add a little red wine and let it evaporate.

When the chorizo is cold, chop it into very small pieces and do the same with the feta.

Mix both together and stuff into the squid. Be careful not to over-stuff or they will split.

Fix a toothpick to close the end then either shallow-fry in oil (with a little butter if you want them to have a golden finish) for 2 or 3 minutes or grill on an oiled grill placed on the barbecue.

Cases & bases

*Blinis make great bases for any smoked fish and caviar. Invite your guests to make their own. Cook the blinis first and the caviar, smoked fish, sour cream and small sprigs of fresh dill can be placed into separate bowls on the table. All it takes is to place some smoked fish, topped with a small spoonful of sour cream, a tiny mound of caviar and a sprig of dill on each blini. These are Russian, so how about drinking them with iced vodka?*

# Blinis with smoked fish and caviar

### *Makes about 20*

1 packet dry yeast (2½ teaspoons) or ¾ oz/25 g fresh yeast

1 level tablespoon lukewarm water

1 level tablespoon sugar

1 cup buckwheat flour

1 cup all-purpose/plain flour

2 cups milk, at room temperature

2 eggs, at room temperature

3 tablespoons unsalted butter, melted

oil, for frying

In a small bowl, combine the yeast with a little lukewarm water, sugar and ¼ cup of the two flours mixed together.

Cover with plastic wrap and let stand in a warm place until bubbly (about 20 minutes). At this stage you can use a food processor with a dough hook.

Combine the yeast mixture and the rest of the flour mixture, the milk and eggs to make a batter (the thickness of pancakes). Add the melted butter last of all and mix gently. Cover the bowl with plastic wrap and let the dough rise in a warm place until doubled in size (about 20–30 minutes).

In a non-stick frying pan, add about 1 tablespoon of oil (I always use extra virgin olive oil but Russians may use vegetable oil or butter). Use medium heat.

When the oil is hot, drop a tablespoon of the batter into the pan and cook until bubbles appear on the surface.

Depending on the size of your frying pan, you can cook more than one blini at a time.

Turn and cook the other side. Once cooked, set aside on a warmed plate in a low oven to keep warm, while you cook the remaining blinis.

*Thin crêpes make good wraps. They can be plain or try adding a teaspoon of crushed dill or caraway seeds to the crepe mixture.*

# Crêpes for smoked fish

*Makes 6–10*

Use a blender to mix together all of the ingredients and make a batter. Rest for about for about 30 minutes before using. Fry in butter or oil.

Place some fish on one side of the crepe. For fillings, try any type of smoked fish, such as salmon or trout, and add some fresh, soft herbs such as cilantro/coriander, dill, fennel or chervil. Dollop in some sour cream or egg mayonnaise then wrap the crepe around the filling.

5 oz/150 g all-purpose/plain flour
1 tablespoon of butter, softened
2 eggs
a pinch of salt
4 fl oz/120 ml milk
butter or oil for frying
smoked fish, such as salmon or trout, for fillings
soft herbs, such as cilantro/coriander, dill, fennel or chervil
sour cream or Mayonnaise (see recipe page 91)

*The friend who gave me this recipe serves these fritters on a large platter topped with smoked fish and a dash of sweet chilli sauce or some sour cream. Any other smoked fish could also be suitable. Gravlax, trout, eel, caviar (the large, pearl variety from Atlantic salmon) or cooked shrimp/prawns also work — try green, cleaned shrimp/prawns sautéed in a little butter with freshly ground pepper and deglazed with a dash of white dry wine. There are many variations for making corn fritters — I like this combination.*

# Corn and herb fritters with smoked fish

*Makes about 12*

5 oz/150 g all-purpose/plain flour
½ teaspoons baking powder
1 teaspoon cumin seeds
½ teaspoon chilli flakes
salt and pepper
4 fl oz/120 ml milk
14 oz/420 g cooked kernels (cut from about 2 or 3 corn cobs), or the equivalent of drained canned corn
2 eggs, separated and the whites whipped to a peak
clarified butter or extra virgin olive oil or a mixture of both

Mix the flour, baking powder, cumin, chilli flakes and salt and pepper.

Add the milk, corn and egg yolks, and combine well. Fold in the whipped egg whites and rest for about 10–15 minutes.

Heat a little clarified butter or extra virgin olive oil or a mixture of both in a non-stick pan and slide large spoonfuls of mixture into the frying pan — the mixture will spread slightly.

Cook for about 3 minutes on each side on moderate heat until golden. Continue until the batter is finished.

Once cooked, set aside and wrap in a kitchen towel or place them on a warmed plate in a low oven to keep warm, while you cook the remaining blinis.

To serve, place a piece of smoked salmon or fish on top of the fritter and garnish with fresh cilantro/coriander.

For a completely different taste, I have also made the above batter and used fresh dill or dill seeds instead of the cumin and chilli. In this option, you can use buttermilk instead of the milk.

# Empanadas

The great thing about empanadas (stuffed pastries) is that they are so versatile. They are generally associated with Spain and come with all sorts of flavours and fillings and they can be baked or fried. But other cuisines have their own versions of empanadas by another name; for example the Turkish have gozleme; the Indians, samosas; and the Italians have calzoni.

The Sicilian version is known as 'Mpanata. The word is closest to the Spanish because Sicily became a colony of Spain in the 16th century. And the Sicilian speciality features swordfish or tuna, although I prefer mackerel or kingfish because they are sustainably fished.

Shapes differ and empanadas can be made into small half moons (empanadillas) or made into large shapes and then cut into slices.

You can make oil pastry (made with bread dough) or use commercial short pastry, including filo pastry (some refer to it as phyllo), but once again this would be even further away from the traditional recipes.

I am embarrassed to say that as an Italian I disapprove when someone suggests using non-traditional ingredients in something that is steeped in so much culture and history. But if you wish to use ready-bought filo pastry you will need to work quickly with it otherwise it dries out—there will be instructions to follow on the packet. The layers are usually brushed with melted butter or oil to help them brown and keep them crispy. Filo pastry can be fried or oven-baked and it cooks very quickly. Bake at 350°F/180°C or fry in hot oil.

Rather than fry my empanadas I prefer to bake them. Here are two recipes, one Spanish, one Sicilian.

*This pastry is derivative of the baronial pastry once made in opulent kitchens during the time that the Spaniards ruled Sicily. The pastry should be compact and not need any extra liquid. But when you are mixing it, if you feel it is too dry to roll out easily, add more butter and egg yolk. Some recipes use a combination of whole eggs and egg yolks, others add a little white wine or lemon juice for the extra moisture. A little water can also be used. The shape can be round or it can be shaped into a large half moon like the empanadas described above.*

# Large 'Mpanata with Sicilian Flavours

## Serves 6–8

Mix the flour, salt, lemon peel and sugar together.

Add the butter and egg yolk. I use my fingers or a blunt knife blade to rub these into the flour. A food processor also works, but do not overwork the pastry—a few short pulses should be sufficient. Add the water (or wine). Add a little more liquid if necessary. The mixture should form into a ball.

Rest the pastry in the fridge for at least 1 hour.

Prepare a tomato salsa with olive oil, tomatoes, onions and garlic. Place all of these ingredients in a pan and cook uncovered until thickened.

Add the fish, cover and braise for about 7–10 minutes (the fish will cook more in the oven).

Add all the other ingredients and allow the mixture to cool.

Divide the pastry in two and roll out into rounds. Make one slightly larger than the other, for the base. At this stage you may wish to place the base onto a piece of baking parchment/paper on a baking tray.

Cover the base with the fish mixture, leaving about ½ in/1 cm around the edge. Cover with the rest of the pastry. Dampen the edges and seal by rolling the edges of the pastry towards the top, pressing together with fingers. Use a knife to slit a few vents into the top. Use a little olive oil to brush the top of the pastry.

Bake the 'Mpanata on 430°F/220°C for about 30–35 minutes until the crust is golden.

### SHORT SWEET PASTRY

10½ oz/300 g plain flour, (durum wheat is preferable)

pinch of salt

grated lemon or/and orange peel from 1 fruit

2 teaspoons sugar

2 oz/50 g butter

1 egg yolk

¼ cup cold water or white wine

2 tablespoons extra virgin olive oil for brushing the pastry

### FILLING

½ cup extra virgin olive oil

4–5 red tomatoes, peeled and chopped

2 large onions, chopped

2–3 cloves garlic, chopped

1lb 9 oz/700 g firm flesh, non-oily fish, cut into large cubes

12 green olives, chopped

2 tablespoons capers

salt and freshly ground pepper

1 tablespoon parsley and basil

1 tablespoon pine nuts

*There are many varieties of canned tuna and sardines. It is worth reading the labels and selecting carefully. You can use fresh or sachet yeast: ⅓ oz/10 g of fresh yeast = 1 teaspoon of dry yeast. These can also be deep fried.*

# Mini empanadas made with canned tuna and harissa

## *Makes about 12*

Dissolve the yeast in a little warm water and add sugar; leave this until it bubbles. Mix in the flour and salt, adding a little warm water as you work the mixture into a firm dough. You can also use a processor with a dough hook.

Sprinkle with a little flour and leave in a bowl covered with plastic wrap or under a tea towel to rise for about 1 hour.

After the dough has risen, add the olive oil gradually and knead again until the oil is totally absorbed.

Meanwhile, prepare the filling. Heat the extra virgin olive oil in a frying pan and sauté the onion.

Add the tomatoes, seasoning, herbs, spices and the garlic. Reduce until the mixture thickens. Cool. Add tomato paste, lemon juice and canned fish last of all.

Divide the pastry into 12 appropriately sized balls; dust with extra flour and roll out the balls into thin round shapes.

Place 1–1½ teaspoons of the filling onto each round to one side. Fold over the pastry and make a semi-circle. Dampen the edges and seal by pressing the edges together; use a fork to seal and to decorate the pastry around the edges.

Prick each empanada or make a small slit in each (only if you are baking them). Glaze with a little extra virgin olive oil.

Place on baking trays lined with greased baking parchment/paper and bake in preheated oven at 430°F/220°C for 15–20 minutes until golden (or fry in hot oil and drain on kitchen paper).

I like to eat these with harissa (recipe page 59).

## PASTRY

⅓ oz/10 g of fresh yeast or 1 teaspoon dried yeast
warm water
1 teaspoon sugar
10½ oz/300 g all-purpose/plain flour, plus extra for rolling
pinch of salt
2 tablespoons extra virgin olive oil plus extra for glazing

## FILLING

2 tablespoons extra virgin olive oil
1 onion, chopped finely
2 tomatoes, diced finely
salt to taste
1 tablespoon fresh chopped parsley or cilantro/coriander
1 teaspoon sweet pimenton
1 pinch hot pimenton
1 teaspoon crushed fennel seeds
2–3 garlic cloves, chopped finely
1 tablespoon tomato paste
1 tablespoon lemon juice
9 oz/250 g can tuna or sardines packed in oil, drained and broken up with a fork

*Harissa is a hot chilli condiment and ingredient and is the favoured national spice of Tunisia, but it is also popular in Algeria and Libya. It is very common to have harissa with couscous. There are now many books about Middle Eastern cuisine with recipes and variations for making it, but this version is very simple. I like to use whole caraway or cumin seeds rather than the powder and I do not usually weigh the chilli flakes, but the following ratio works well. In Tunisia they use a dry, very dark whole chilli that produces a harissa with an intense colour.*

# Harissa

### *Makes about 9 fl oz/250 ml*

Pour hot water on to the chilli flakes (just enough to cover them) and soak for about 30 minutes. If using caraway seeds rather than powder, add these to soak as well. (The water will be absorbed and the flakes should swell.)

Blend the ingredients in a small food processor.

Add the garlic, salt and some the extra virgin olive oil. You may need to add a little water—the mixture should resemble a soft paste.

Pack into small glass jars and top with oil to seal. Replace the oil covering each time you use the harissa.

When I visited Tunis, oil flavoured with harissa was often served in the restaurants as a dip. This was accompanied with fresh bread. To make harissa, flavoured oil, mix one tablespoon of harissa with three tablespoons of extra virgin olive oil. Stir it before use.

hot water, to soften the chilli
5 oz/150 g dried chilli flakes
1 tablespoon whole caraway or cumin seeds
4–5 garlic cloves, minced
salt, 1 tablespoon
extra virgin olive oil, ½ cup for the mixture and a little extra to seal

*I often buy a whole smoked trout and I always peel the skin back from one side when I present it to expose the flesh and make it easier to serve. I also use the leftover trout to make a log, either in a thick strip or just the shredded flesh mixed with some cream cheese (I like quark) and some thick cream or mascarpone. If horseradish is in season, try grating it on top rather than adding it to the filling. The asparagus is optional but it does look good when the log is sliced. Brown bread or pumpernickel goes well with this. You could try serving this with finely shredded cooked beetroot dressed with leftover cream cheese mixture thinned with a little cream and horseradish as an accompaniment.*

# Log of smoked trout wrapped in smoked salmon and silverbeet

### Serves 6–8

Rinse the silverbeet and remove the thick white stalks.

Cook the silverbeet leaves. I usually cook them in a little salted water, drain them and then lay on kitchen paper to absorb further moisture.

Mix the cream cheese with the cream or mascarpone. Using a wooden spoon, beat in the horseradish, lemon juice, pepper, chives and capers.

On a piece of plastic wrap, place a single layer of whole cooked silverbeet leaves. You may not need to use all four leaves but they come in useful in case you need to patch up holes. I usually drizzle a little extra virgin olive oil, salt, pepper and a little lemon juice to dress the leaves.

Top with a very thin layer of cream cheese mixture. Place a layer of smoked salmon on top of the cream cheese. Repeat with a very thin layer of cream cheese mixture. Add a thick strip, or shreds, of smoked trout in the centre. Lay some cooked asparagus spears on either side. Cover with more cream cheese mixture.

Use the plastic wrap to roll the layers into a neat log. Use the extra leaves of silverbeet if necessary. Press it firmly together so that the different layers stick. Leave for at least an hour or overnight in the refrigerator to set.

Slice and serve.

3–4 large silverbeet leaves (also called chard), cooked, left whole

9 oz/250 g cream cheese,

a little cream or mascarpone, enough to make the cream cheese spreadable

1 teaspoon fresh horseradish, finely grated, or prepared horseradish

juice of 1 lemon

black or pink pepper, coarsely ground

1 tablespoon chives or scallions/ spring onions, thinly sliced

1 tablespoon capers

extra virgin olive oil, salt, pepper and a little lemon juice, for dressing (optional)

a little extra olive oil, sal

5–6 slices smoked salmon

smoked trout fillet skinned, boned

4 asparagus spears, cooked

In many bars in railway stations in north Italy you are likely to find small triangular sandwiches made from two slices of soft white bread with the crust removed. Tramezzo means 'in between', and in between the bread you will find a variety of fillings. Do not overstuff them or cut the bread too thickly—you need to get your mouth around the three layers of bread and two of the fillings pressed together. They are usually made with white bread but they can look attractive with dark or grainy bread for one of the slices. Tramezzini are great for picnics and casual lunches. My favourites as a child were layers of Russian Salad (Insalata Russa) (see recipe page 89) and tinned tuna.

# Double-decker sandwiches
## Tramezzini
### Makes 12

18 slices of square bread, crusts cut off
Russian Salad (see recipe page 89)
unsalted butter, to spread on the bread (this is optional but it does help the bread and the filling to stick together)
tinned tuna, packed in oil and drained
12 small artichokes under oil, drained and sliced thinly

For the bottom layer of bread, spread about 1 tablespoon of Insalata Russa over 1 slice. Butter a new slice of bread on one side and cover the Insalate Russa.

For the second and top layer: place a little drained, flaked canned tuna and a few slices of artichokes.

Butter another slice of bread and cover the stack with it(you will have three slices of bread altogether).

Repeat the process with the remaining bread slices and fillings.

Cut each diagonally into two halves to make two triangles.

ALTERNATIVE FILLINGS
For the first and bottom layer: butter the bread and use some cooked and chopped shrimp/prawns or smoked trout or smoked salmon on the bread. Top with some finely shredded lettuce and some mayonnaise. Cover with a new slice of bread and butter it.

For the second and top layer: use some slices of black or green olives and slices of hard-boiled eggs, slices of avocado or thin cooked asparagus dipped in lemon juice with a drizzle of olive oil and freshly ground black pepper on top.

Continue as above.

*This was another favourite* spuntino *(small bite) in my household when I first left Italy. While my friends' mothers were making stuffed curried eggs, my mum was making these.*

# Stuffed eggs with anchovies

*Serves 3*

Cut hardboiled eggs in half, lengthways.

Remove the yolks.

Mash the yolks and combine with the other ingredients except the capers.

Refill the eggs with the mixture and decorate with a caper.

You could also stuff eggs with the Russian Salad (see recipe page 89). Proceed as above, but mix minced egg yolks with the Russian Salad. Fill the eggs and top them with some flaked tuna or a small cooked shrimp or an anchovy fillet.

6 hard-boiled eggs

STUFFING MIX

1 tablespoon Italian parsley, finely chopped

1 garlic clove, mashed

4 anchovy fillets (to taste)

1 tablespoon extra virgin olive oil or egg mayonnaise

1 tablespoon capers

# Pizza

There is something about the smell of pizza that makes you want to eat me. And pizzas are so versatile—you can make them any size, large or small. If I make pizza, I always make my own dough. However, there are ready-made bases that you can buy, including gluten-free ones. Italian bakers will sell you unbaked bread dough that you can than shape to the size of your choice.

Pizzas originated in Naples and are now eaten all over the world. Keep in mind that the bases of traditional pizzas are thin (not thick) and they are not heaped with large amounts of toppings. They should cook quickly and be crisp and crusty. If you are making one large pizza or small pizzas for 6–8 people, the quantities I have listed for each recipe are sufficient.

## pizza dough

12 oz/350 g strong '00' flour • 7 fl oz/200–210 ml warm water • 1 sachet dried yeast (If using compressed yeast, 10g of fresh yeast equals 1 teaspoon of dried yeast and there are about 2½ teaspoons in a sachet) • ½ teaspoon sugar • ½ teaspoon salt • 1 tablespoon extra virgin olive oil

Dissolve the yeast in half of the warm water. Add the sugar and leave in a warm place for 10 minutes, until the mixture is frothy and bubbly.

Mix flour and salt and the rest of the warm water to form the dough. Different flours have different degrees of absorption so add the water slowly as you may need a little less or a little more of water. Knead until the dough is smooth and elastic. Rest in warm place in a bowl covered with plastic wrap for at least 1 hour or until doubled in size.

Knead it lightly again, work in the oil, divide the dough into the number of pizzas you want and roll the dough out to a thickness of about ¼ in/5 mm.

*Shelled, green shrimp/prawns are also a good substitute. Strange as it seems, potatoes are often added to this pizza in the Italian region of Campania.*

# pizza with mussels

## Pizza alle cozze
### Serves 8

Preheat the oven to 480°F/250°C.

Make pizza dough as listed on page 64. Divide dough into 8 balls and roll out to make small pizzas (thickness about ¼ in/5 mm). Lay out your pizza bases onto baking trays lined with oiled baking parchment/paper.

Heat up the olive oil in a pan and sauté the parsley and garlic for about 20 seconds.

Add the potatoes and toss them around in the hot oil, before adding mussel meat. Keep stirring the ingredients until fragrant and well coated.

Arrange the filling on the bases, top with ricotta and tomatoes.

Grind salt and pepper on top of the tomatoes and a drizzle extra virgin olive oil all over the pizzas.

Bake in the oven for about 15 minutes. Swap position of trays halfway through cooking.

3 tablespoons extra virgin olive oil

2 tablespoons fresh parsley

2–3 cloves of garlic, finely chopped

2 medium-sized potatoes, cooked, peeled and cut into small cubes

9 oz/250 g mussel meat or shrimp/prawns

5 oz/150 g ricotta, drained

2–3 very ripe tomatoes, cut into small cubes

salt and freshly ground black pepper

extra virgin olive oil, to drizzle

*Pissaladière is usually referred to as French pizza. It is usually made on a bread dough base, but it can also be made with a shortcrust or puff pastry base. For a dough base see the recipe on page 64. Roll the bread dough out to a thickness of ¼ in/5 mm. Use a square or rectangular-shaped baking sheet/pan if you are using the sheets of readymade pastry This is a dish designed for people who love anchovies. If you like, chop the anchovies and fry in a little oil until they disintegrate, then mix with the onion. Some cooks soak the anchovies in milk for about an hour beforehand; this removes some of the salt. In this recipe, the onions are cooked slowly so you get the sweetness of the onions set against the saltiness of the anchovies and black olives.*

# A French pizza with anchovies

## Pissaladière or pissaladiera niçoise
### Serves 4

Place the onions in a pan with the olive oil and white wine.

Add seasoning and herbs, cover and simmer over low heat for 20 minutes.

Add the teaspoon of sugar (optional) to the onions.

The onions should be soft but not browned. There should not be any moisture at the bottom of the pan. Cool.

Preheat the oven to 400–430°F/200–220°C.

Place a sheet of pastry into a baking tray lined with baking parchment/paper. If using homemade dough, roll out ¾ of the dough into a square or rectangular shape. Reserve the remaining dough for the lattice work.

Cover the sheet of pastry with the cooked onions (remove the herbs). Spread the onions out evenly over the dough. Arrange anchovies on top in a regular criss-cross pattern to create a diamond shape and place an olive in the centre of each diamond.

Cut strips of the other sheet of pastry into long and even thin strips and make decorative squares (lattice-work) over the surface. If using homemade dough, roll the dough flat and then cut into long strips.

Bake for about 20–25 minutes until the edges of the dough are golden brown.

Serve it hot, warm or cold. Cut it into square shapes.

18 oz/500g onions, thinly sliced

3 tablespoons extra virgin olive oil

1 tablespoon white wine

salt and freshly ground black pepper

fresh thyme or rosemary sprigs or bay leaves (in the style of Provence)

1 teaspoon sugar (optional)

12 or more anchovy fillets, good quality, canned in oil (they can also be cut in half vertically

18 black olives

2 ready rolled sheets of commercial shortcrust pastry or homemade dough

# pizza with onion and anchovy

## Pizza alle cipolle e acciughe

*Serves 6–8*

3 tablespoons extra virgin olive oil

2 large red onions, sliced into rings

2–3 very ripe tomatoes, cut into small cubes

24 pitted black olives

2 tablespoons parsley, finely chopped

24 capers, or more, to taste

salt and freshly ground black pepper, to taste

1 handful basil leaves

12–18 anchovy fillets, to taste

7 oz/200 g fresh mozzarella or bocconcini cheese, sliced

Make pizza dough as described on page 64.

Divide dough into 6–8 balls and roll out to make small pizzas (thickness about ¼ in/5 mm).

Heat the oil and sauté the onion rings until soft. Add the remaining ingredients except for the anchovies, basil leaves and cheese.

Sprinkle half of the torn basil leaves onto the bases, top with the mixture, and decorate with anchovies, slices of the cheese and the rest of the torn basil leaves. Follow the instructions for baking as in the recipe Pizza with Mussels (page 65).

*These little fried, round pizze (plural of pizza) are popular all over Italy. Once fried, they are usually topped with a little tomato salsa, some grated Parmesan or pecorino cheese, a basil leaf and an anchovy. Instead of the traditional salsa I also sometimes like to use wilted cherry tomatoes.*

# Mini fried pizze

## Pizzette
### *Makes 20–24 pizzette (mini-pizze)*

DOUGH • ⅓ oz/10 g fresh, compressed yeast or 1 tablespoon dry yeast • about 6fl oz/175ml warm water • ½ teaspoon sugar • 9 oz/250 g plain flour • ½ teaspoon salt • 1 tablespoon extra virgin olive oil

TOMATO SALSA • ½ onion, sliced finely • 2 tablespoons extra virgin olive oil • fresh basil leaves • salt to taste • 5 red tomatoes, peeled (or use canned tomatoes)

WILTED CHERRY TOMATOES • cherry tomatoes, cut in half • extra virgin olive oil • salt and pepper, to taste • 1 clove garlic, crushed • fresh thyme, basil or oregano, to taste

TOPPINGS • 1 teaspoon tomato salsa or 1 wilted cherry tomato per mini pizza • 1 salted anchovy on each • about ½ teaspoon grated Parmesan or pecorino cheese • fresh basil leaves

Make the dough using the method for pizza dough on page 64. There will be more bubbles in the pizzette when you fry them because there is more yeast.

To make the tomato salsa, place everything in a pan and reduce until cooked.

Wilt the cherry tomatoes by lightly frying them, cut side down, in a little extra virgin olive oil. Season and add crushed garlic. Mix in the fresh herbs and take off the heat.

Shape the dough into small egg-shaped lumps and flatten with your fingers that have been dipped in olive oil (about ¼ in/5 mm thick). Or use a rolling pin and cut into squares or crescent shapes.

Fry the pizzette in abundant, very hot extra virgin olive oil, 2–3 at a time. As they swell, flip them over. They will cook quickly. Dry on kitchen paper. Top with salsa or the tomatoes, an anchovy, grated cheese and a basil leaf.

*What is great about making rice paper rolls is that you can put almost anything in them—and the ingredients do not have to be Vietnamese. I often use long thin strips of zucchini/courgette or red bell peppers/capsicum instead of cucumbers, and basil instead of Thai basil or Vietnamese mint. Vietnamese cooks may not approve!*

*I use crabmeat or/and shrimp/prawns as the seafood. You can also easily omit the seafood from the particular rice paper rolls that you present to vegetarian friends. In a restaurant in Hoi An, I was shown how to add passionfruit to rice paper rolls. This may sound strange but it adds a tart and tangy taste.*

# Rice paper rolls with dipping sauces

USE ANY COMBINATION OF THE FOLLOWING shrimp/prawns • crabmeat fresh • Thai basil • fresh mint leaves • fresh cilantro/coriander leaves • garlic chives • rice vermicelli lettuce leaves (use soft lettuce), cut into fine ribbons or use a whole leaf and place this as your first layer on top of the rice paper • mung bean sprouts • carrots, grated • cucumbers, peeled and cut into long thin strips • chillies, stemmed, halved, seeds removed, and thinly sliced lengthwise • use the green and white part of scallions/spring onions, quartered lengthwise and cut into strips • passionfruit pulp (optional)

A SAMPLE RECIPE • 6 rice paper wrappers • 6–12 medium-sized or large cooked shrimp/prawns, peeled, deveined and cut in half • 7 oz/200 g vermicelli rice noodles, dipped in boiling water for 4–5 minutes and drained • a handful of fresh cilantro/coriander leaves and a handful of fresh mint leaves • 4 soft lettuce leaves, shredded • 1–2 small scallions/spring onions cut into long, thin strips • 6 strips cucumber, peeled and cut into long, thin strips

Prepare all of your ingredients and have them ready in separate piles.

Dip each sheet of rice paper into a bowl of warm water. Do this one at a time and quickly or they may break (about 15 seconds).

Place 6 wrappers flat on a clean, slightly damp cloth.

To prepare the rolls, I like to work on one rice paper sheet at a time. Take one of the sheets, lay it flat on a clean surface and work quickly. Place some of the lettuce on first, then the herbs. Leave a ¾ in/2 cm border around the edges.

Next, place some of the vermicelli rice noodles in a long, narrow line down the centre of the wrapper.

Place the shrimp/prawns next in the centre, then the cucumber and the scallions.

Make sure the filling is compact and slowly roll wrapper into a cylinder: roll the wrapper halfway into the centre, tuck the edges of the rice paper into the filling and finish rolling.

To seal the roll, gently dab some warm water on the edge—it should stick together. Repeat the process with the remaining sheets of rice paper and ingredients. Cover with cling film to stop the rolls drying out. Serve with one of the dipping sauces.

PINEAPPLE DIPPING SAUCE • 1 cup unsweetened pineapple juice • pinch of salt • 1 tablespoon vinegar • 1 tablespoon palm sugar, grated • ½ teaspoon cornstarch/cornflour

In a small bowl, combine the pineapple juice, salt, vinegar and sugar. Whisk in the cornstarch.
   Place the mixture into a small saucepan and cook slowly, stirring often, until the sauce thickens. Cool.

CUMQUAT AND SOY DIPPING SAUCE • 4–6 cumquats • 1 tablespoon soy sauce • a dash of vegetable oil or sesame oil

*There are many combinations you can use for a dipping sauce. When cumquats are in season, my daughter uses this one.*

Cut 3 cumquats in half, remove the seeds and squeeze the juice into a small bowl.
   Add the soy sauce and oil and mix it together.
   Cut the last cumquat into thin slices and add it to the mixture.

A SIMPLE DIPPING SAUCE • zest and juice of 1 lime • 1 teaspoon fish sauce • 1 teaspoon rice vinegar • 1 teaspoon superfine/caster sugar • 1 teaspoon roasted peanuts, finely chopped • 1 small red chilli, cut into rings (leave the seeds in if you like it hot)

Mix all the ingredients together.

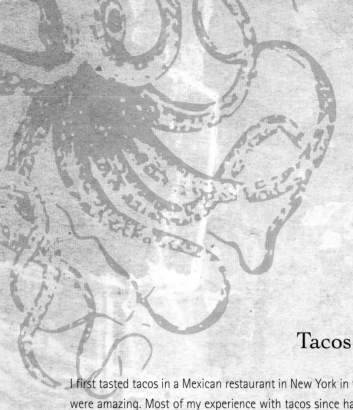

# Tacos

I first tasted tacos in a Mexican restaurant in New York in the 1970s and the varieties this restaurant had were amazing. Most of my experience with tacos since has been limited to refried beans and meat, and it is only recently that I have eaten and made crab tacos and fish tacos—I have a new American friend.

The tortilla is the shell. The taco is all the shell and filling. The hard tortilla shells are generally made with white corn or yellow corn. The soft tortillas are generally made with white flour.

The instructions for heating the tortillas are on the packet. Some can be heated in an oiled pan, others fried or warmed in the oven.

I like to let my guests to assemble their own. I put the warm tortillas, one or more of the salsas and one or more of the fish fillings—battered or lightly floured and fried fish, or fish cakes made with crab or flaked fish or raw fish that has been marinating in fresh lime juice—in separate plates or bowls on the table and invite my guests to roll up their sleeves and hop in.

To assemble the tacos, grab a tortilla, place some filling on it, add the salsa and roll it together. If you think that this procedure is a little unrefined you can use a toothpick to hold the tacos that you have assembled and serve.

I prefer to use the soft, small tortillas for making any of the crab and fish tacos.

*If you are planning to buy fresh crabs, remember that they are seasonal. If you are using frozen or canned crabmeat, drain it beforehand.*

# Crab tacos
## Makes 6

Sauté the onions in some butter or extra virgin olive oil (or a mixture of the two). When the onion begins to soften, add the crabmeat.

Add some salt, fresh chilli, spice, garlic and cilantro. Cook it for about 7–10 minutes.

Take the crab mixture out of the pan and, if there are juices there, do not waste them: evaporate the juices and turn them into a glaze.

Return the cooked crabmeat to the pan and mix together. The mixture should keep warm in the pan until you are ready to serve. Add your choice of salsas and fillings, as listed on page 74.

2 onions, finely chopped
21 oz/600 g crabmeat, fresh, canned or frozen, defrosted and well drained
butter or extra virgin olive oil
salt
1 chilli, seeds removed and finely chopped
½–1 teaspoon ground cumin
2 cloves garlic, finely chopped
cilantro/coriander, finely chopped, to garnish
salt to taste
6 soft, small tortillas

# Fish tacos
## Makes 6

Lightly fry or batter the fish you are using (use any of the batters in the Floured, Crumbed and Battered chapter).

Warm the corn tortillas in a hot, oiled frying pan.

Add whatever salsas or fillings you prefer from the recipes over the page. With fish tacos, I like to use guacamole and I top the fish with some cabbage salad. To make the cabbage salad, combine all of the ingredients together.

Alternatively, use just the tomato salsa (see Salsas and Fillings on page 74) as the topping for the fish. The olive oil is optional and not traditional.

6 pieces of fish
6 soft, small tortillas
olive oil, for frying

CABBAGE SALAD
1 cup red or white cabbage, very finely shredded
salt and pepper to taste
juice of 1 lemon
1 tablespoon extra virgin olive oil

# Salsas and fillings

*All recipes make enough for 6 tacos*

MANGO SALSA • 1 cup mango flesh, cubed • ½ cup cilantro/coriander, chopped • juice of 1 lime (or lemon) • 1 scallion/spring onion or red onion, finely sliced for colour • salt and pepper or chilli flakes, to taste • 1 tablespoon extra virgin olive oil • 1 avocado, cubed (optional)

Mix all the ingredients together in a bowl. If using avocado, add it to the mango salsa just before you serve it, so that it doesn't discolour.

GUACAMOLE • 1 cup avocados, mashed • salt • Serrano chillies (or use fresh chillies) • ½ cup chopped cilantro/coriander • juice of 1 lime (or lemon) • sprinkle of cumin • 2 garlic cloves, minced • 1 scallion/spring onion, finely chopped • 1 small green tomato, diced • 1 tablespoon extra virgin olive oil

Mix all the ingredients together in a bowl.

TOMATO SALSA • 7 oz/200 g tomatoes (about 2) • ½ cup finely chopped cilantro/coriander • 1 scallion/spring onion (or 1 tablespoon red onion), finely sliced • a splash of extra virgin olive oil • salt and pepper • 1 small pale stalk from the centre of a stick of celery and its soft leaves, very finely chopped

A salsa that can go well with the fish can be made with fresh tomatoes.

Slice the tomatoes in half and then dice the halves. If the tomatoes are particularly juicy, you may wish to drain off some of the tomato liquid before placing the diced tomato into a bowl.

Add the rest of the ingredients into the bowl and toss to combine.

*A friend of mine grows different varieties of lettuces and a large variety of herbs. And she always has two key ingredients in her refrigerator—white anchovies preserved in oil and a container of homemade, oven-dried tomatoes, covered in extra virgin olive oil so she can make this impressive appetiser at short notice. Sun-dried tomatoes can be used as a substitute but the oven-dried ones are far more delectable with a more intense flavour, and they are really simple to make. Leaves and herbs for this appetiser can change with the seasons. White anchovies are available from good delicatessens/providores. If you'd like to give an extra zing to white anchovies, see the recipe for Zucchini and mint fritters on page 192.*

# White anchovy and oven-dried tomato leaf boats

salad leaves that have a small boat shape, such as witlof, chicory, radicchio, baby cos
chives
white anchovies
oven-dried tomatoes (see recipe below)
extra virgin olive oil
cracked black pepper

### OVEN-DRIED TOMATOES
15–20 small to medium-sized tomatoes
sprigs of fresh thyme, chopped
extra virgin olive oil
cracked black pepper
sea salt flakes

Wash and pat dry the selected leaves for the 'boats'.

Wash and slice the chives into ½ in/1 cm lengths.

One anchovy fillet and half an oven-dried tomato are required for each leaf.

Soak up the preserving oil on the anchovies with paper towel. Do the same with the oven-dried tomatoes.

Arrange the leaves on a serving platter. Depending on the size of your tomatoes and of the leaves, place one to three halves on each leaf. Drape an anchovy fillet over the tomatoes. Scatter chopped chives over the leaves.

Drizzle each with extra virgin olive oil and sprinkle with cracked black pepper.

To oven-dry the tomatoes, halve the tomatoes, scoop out the seeds and place, cup side up, on an oven tray. Drizzle with extra virgin olive oil. Sprinkle with salt, pepper and thyme.

Slowly dry in a 285°F/140°C oven for several hours. They should still be plump and moist and not completely dry or browned.

When cool, place in a lidded glass container. Cover with extra virgin olive oil. Make sure they are completely submerged. Refrigerate until required—they'll keep this way for a few weeks.

It is not difficult to imagine how these tomatoes would enhance other recipes in this book. For example, try them in the fish sliders recipes from page 194.

soused & best dressed

*This soup is traditionally served with white grapes. Try it instead with cooked shrimp/prawns cut into small pieces and serve it in teacups or glasses. I once served this soup in a large tureen with fresh rose petals scattered on top. They are edible and look spectacular.*

# Cold almond soup with small cooked shrimp

## Serves 6

Place bread in 1–2 cups cold water to soak for 5 minutes. Drain and squeeze out as much water as you can.

Place almonds into a food processor and grind until pulverised. Add garlic, seasoning and bread, and pulse.

Drizzle extra virgin olive oil into the mixture, then vinegar (like when making a mayonnaise). The mixture should be smooth and thick.

Finally thin out the mixture with the stock. Add more stock or water if you would like a thinner soup.

Refrigerate and serve very cold.

Taste it for seasoning and adjust if necessary, as cold dishes usually require more seasoning than hot dishes.

Add minced shrimp when ready to serve.

2 slices white bread, use good quality sourdough, crusts removed

5 oz/150 g almonds, blanched, peeled and set aside to dry on kitchen paper

2–3 cloves garlic, peeled and cut finely

salt and black pepper, to taste

¼ cup extra virgin olive oil

1 tablespoon sherry or champagne vinegar, or good quality white wine vinegar

3 cups chicken stock

6 tablespoons cooked shrimp/prawns, cut into very small pieces or coarsely minced

*This recipe for cold soup is particularly refreshing on a hot day. But this is no ordinary soup. I add something delectable to the soup by sprinkling the surface with plump, flavourful balls of red caviar that pop in the mouth. If you aren't able to buy this caviar, any caviar will do, or add a raw oyster topped with a squeeze of lemon. Use either Lebanese or small cucumbers (fewer seeds). I like to serve these in coffee cups or glasses.*

# Green cucumber gazpacho with caviar

## Serves 6

2 cups cucumbers, peeled and cubed (remove some of the seeds if there are too many)

½ cup pale green centre leaves of green celery

1–2 cloves garlic, minced

1 tablespoon fresh lemon juice or sherry vinegar (less harsh than wine vinegar)

2 tablespoons extra virgin olive oil and some extra to drizzle on top

salt and freshly ground black pepper to taste

handful of dill, chopped

2 oz/50 g caviar from Atlantic salmon, to decorate the soup

Place all the ingredients, except the dill and caviar, into a food processor and blend the mixture until smooth. Add the dill and stir through.

Use a little ice-cold water to thin down the soup, if you wish until you have the preferred consistency.

Keep it in the fridge until ready to use.

Place into small coffee cups or glasses and drizzle with a little extra olive oil. Decorate with a sprinkle of caviar or place into a large bowl and sprinkle caviar on top. For this option include a small ladle and some small bowls. Guests can help themselves.

# Fish and leaf salad

Any leftover fish will add more complex tastes to salads—stir-fried, braised or steamed, whatever
cooked fish you have as a leftover—can be used to make a great salad.

If you do not have any ready-cooked fish, it is easy to blanch fish or cleaned squid, which has been cut
into bite-sized pieces scored with criss-cross cuts (use a serrated knife). You can also use cleaned, green
shrimp/prawns or scallops. Instead of blanching the seafood you can sauté it in a little extra virgin olive
oil and garlic.

I enjoy balanced food and am passionate about salad greens and vegetables. Combine the fish or
shellfish with salad vegetables and an Italian or Asian dressing. Select a ratio that suits your taste.

# Poached fish

about 17½oz/500 g thick, white, firmly textured fish or salmon • salt • 3–4 whole peppercorns • bay leaf

Cut your fish pieces into portions about 3 in/8 cm long.

Chose a saucepan with enough room to cover the fish with water. Estimate the amount of liquid you'll need to just cover the fish. Bring the liquid to a simmer; add in the seasonings.

Add the fish; if it has skin, place the fish skin side down. Ensure that the liquid remains at a gentle simmer and does not boil. Poach for 5–7 minutes. Turn off the heat and leave it: the fish is done when the flesh is opaque.

For other seafood, follow the same procedure, but cook the seafood for about 90 seconds. If the seafood needs more cooking, turn off the heat and leave it in the water until the squid turns opaque, the shrimp/prawns have a red tinge and the scallops are set. Drain and let cool.

*The salad dressing is sufficient for a salad made of fish and 7–9 oz/200–250 g of salad.*

# Salad with Asian flavours

scallions/spring onions, finely sliced • herbs: cilantro/coriander, mint and Thai basil leaves • fresh ginger, grated • cucumber, deseeded and cut into strips • chilli • bean sprouts, finely diced • a combination of Asian Greens or any leafy greens or salad leaves torn into bite-sized pieces • lemongrass, very finely sliced • Vietnamese mint (*rau ram* in Thailand; it is called *phak pha* in Malaysia and in Singapore it is called *daun kesom* or *daun laksa*) • young kaffir lime leaves • minced garlic • roasted peanuts • sliced mango or green papaya • green soya beans—I buy them frozen and blanch them to soften them • flowers from chives or purple basil

DRESSING • ½ cup extra virgin olive oil • 1 tablespoon sesame oil • dash fish sauce • lime or lemon juice from 1 fruit • ½ teaspoon sugar • 1–2 passionfruit pulp

Use a selection of ingredients from the list, using whatever is in season or to hand. Select a mixture of bitter and sweet salad leaves of different colours and textures.

Whisk all of the dressing ingredients together in a bowl.

In a large salad bowl, mix together your selection of ingredients and some poached fish (either leftover poached fish or refer to the recipe above). Drizzle over the dressing and serve immediately.

# Salad with Italian flavours

use sturdy textured leaves, with a slightly bitter taste: frisée, radicchio, chicory, batavia, endives, escarole and puntarelle (chicory shoots): all are very suitable ingredients for this salad • pungent greens, like watercress and rocket • sweet-tasting leaves like lamb's lettuce or oak and butter lettuces • fennel, finely sliced • young stalks and leaves of celery • fresh herbs • pulses: cooked borlotti beans or cannellini beans • nasturtium flowers and their young, round leaves • fruit, such as a couple of slices of yellow peaches, blood orange or fresh figs

DRESSING • 3 parts extra virgin olive oil • garlic • freshly ground pepper and salt • 1 part lemon juice or white wine vinegar

Use a selection of ingredients from the list, using whatever is in season or to hand. Select a mixture of bitter and sweet salad leaves of different colours and textures.

Whisk all of the dressing ingredients together in a bowl.

In a large salad bowl, mix together your selection of ingredients and some flaked, poached fish (either leftover poached fish or refer to the recipe on page 85). Drizzle over the dressing and serve immediately.

In spring, I may add vegetables such as fresh uncooked fava broad beans, asparagus, peas, radish or cooked green beans. In summer, I may add strips of roasted bell peppers/capsicums, strips of grilled eggplants/aubergine. In winter, I may add some roasted vegetables, such as pumpkin, beetroot or garlic cloves.

*Helping my mother make this dish was my job as a child. It was a reliable appetiser served on special occasions. Insalata Russa is made with cooked vegetables, cut into small cubes and smothered with homemade egg mayonnaise. It is decorated with hard-boiled eggs, stuffed green olives and canned tuna. Sometimes my mother used some small cooked shrimp/prawns. Ensaladilla Rusa is the Spanish version of this salad and it is a very common tapas dish. The Spaniards make it the same way, but the canned tuna is often mixed in the salad rather than being placed on top. Making it with my mother, we never weighed our ingredients, but the following combination and ratios should please anyone's palate.*

# Russian salad

## Insalata Russa
### Serves 6

Cook potatoes and carrots in their skins in separate pans; cool, peel and cut them into small cubes.

Cook the peas and beans separately, by either steaming them or cooking them in some boiling salted water; drain and cool.

Cut the *giardiniera* into small pieces (carrots, turnips, cauliflower, gherkins).

Mix all of these ingredients together, add the cubed hard-boiled eggs and about 7 oz/200 g of the flaked tuna and a cup of homemade egg mayonnaise (see recipe on page 91).

Level out the Russian salad either on a flat plate or in a bowl and leave in the refrigerator for at least an hour before decorating it by covering it with the remaining mayonnaise.

Have a good old time placing on the top slices of hard-boiled eggs, the rest of the drained tuna or use 3–6 small cooked prawns. Bits of *giardiniera* will also add colour.

2–3 medium-sized potatoes (waxy are best)

3 carrots

1 cup shelled peas

¾–1 cup green beans, cut into ¼ in/1 cm pieces

3 hard-boiled eggs, 2 eggs peeled and cubed and 1 egg, peeled and sliced to decorate the top

½ cup Italian *giardinieria* (mixed garden pickled vegetables, such as carrots, turnips, cauliflower, gherkins, in vinegar)

1½ cups Mayonnaise (see recipe on page 91)

10½ oz/300 g canned tuna, packed in olive oil, drained

salt

*I use a food processor or a stick blender to make mayonnaise. If you are not making the traditional Italian version, it is common to add vinegar instead of lemon juice and a teaspoon of Dijon mustard. As an alternative, the Spaniards like to add a little saffron (pre-softened in a little warm water), to make saffron mayonnaise.*

# Mayonnaise

## *Makes about 12 fl oz/350 ml*

Mix the egg with a little salt in the blender or food processor, or in a clean jar (if using the stick blender).

Slowly add the extra virgin olive oil in a thin, steady stream through the feed tube while the blender or processor is running.

Before adding additional oil, ensure that the oil that has already been added has been incorporated completely.

Add a tablespoon of fresh lemon juice when the mayonnaise is creamy.

1 egg
1–1 ½ cups extra virgin olive oil
1 tablespoon lemon juice

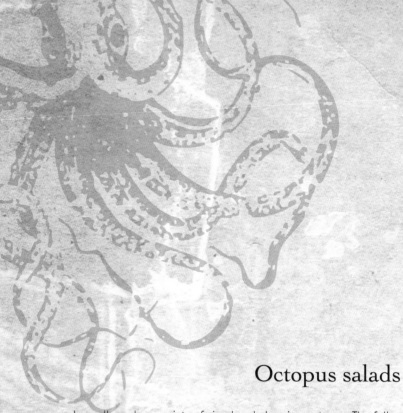

# Octopus salads

I usually make a variety of simple salads using octopus. The following combinations are quite different from one another and reflect the different cuisines from three different Mediterranean cultures. Use the recipe below to prepare your octopus. Then use the cooked octopus in the salad of your choice.

Octopus shrinks, so I prefer to buy large tentacles rather than a whole octopus or lots of baby octopuses, but the choice is yours.

## Cooked octopus

*Serves 6–8*

70 oz/2 kg octopus tentacles • pinch of salt

Place the octopus tentacles in a saucepan and cover them with cold water. Bring slowly to the boil, add the salt and allow to simmer for about 5–10 minutes.

Turn off the heat and leave the octopus in the water for an extra 15 minutes to finish cooking.

Drain the octopus and remove any dark skin or large suckers.

Slice the octopus into chunks and place it in a serving bowl ready to be dressed.

*Cooked octopus (see recipe page 92) is combined with either Italian or Sicilian flavour combinations.*

# Octopus salad with Italian flavours

## Serves 6–8

1 quantity Cooked Octopus (see recipe on page 92 )

In a large bowl, toss the cooked octopus together with the dressing of your choice (recipes following).

SIMPLE ITALIAN SALAD DRESSING • ½ cup fresh lemon juice (with a dash of wine vinegar, optional) • ½ cup extra virgin olive oil • 2 tablespoons finely chopped parsley • 1–2 cloves garlic, chopped • salt and freshly ground black pepper, to taste

Combine all of the ingredients for the dressing in a bowl and whisk together.

SIMPLE SICILIAN DRESSING • ½ cup fresh lemon juice (with a dash of wine vinegar, optional) • ½ cup extra virgin olive oil • 2 tablespoons finely chopped parsley • 1–2 cloves garlic, chopped • salt and freshly ground black pepper, to taste • 1–2 raw peeled carrots, sliced into very thin rounds • 1–2 celery stalks, the light green ones from the centre of the celery and some of the tender leaves, finely chopped • 12 green olives • 2 tablespoons chopped mint or oregano instead of parsley

In a bowl, whisk together the lemon juice, olive oil, parsley, garlic and season to taste. Stir in the carrot and celery, olives and herbs.

# Octopus salad with Middle Eastern flavours

*Serves 6–8*

In a large bowl, combine the cooked octopus, scallions, bell pepper, orange segments, pomegranate seeds and herbs. Gently mix all of the salad ingredients together.

Drizzle the salad dressing (recipe below) over the salad, toss everything together and serve.

SIMPLE SALAD DRESSING • ½ cup fresh lemon juice • ½ cup extra virgin olive oil • 2 teaspoons pomegranate molasses • 1–2 cloves garlic, chopped • 1 teaspoon whole or ground fennel seeds or cumin seeds or a combination of both • 1 tablespoon finely chopped fresh cilantro/coriander • salt and freshly ground black pepper, to taste • 14 oz/400 g cooked garbanzo beans/chickpeas

In a separate bowl, combine the Simple Salad Dressing ingredients.

Photos overleaf.

1 quantity Cooked Octopus (see recipe page 92)

2 scallions/spring onions, finely chopped or 1 red onion, finely sliced

1 red or yellow bell pepper/ capsicum, cut into fine strips (or use roasted or grilled bell peppers/capsicums, see recipe page 98)

1 orange, peeled and cut into slices

½ cup pomegranate seeds (optional)

12 fresh mint leaves or ½ cup of cilantro/coriander leaves

*In Spain, the south of France and in Italy, potatoes and garlic mayonnaise are often added to octopus salad. I also like to add black olives and roast peppers to mine. In Italy, bell peppers are always cooked whole to preserve the taste and juices, and they acquire a unique flavour when placed over a flame or direct heat. The peppers, once peeled, are never rinsed as this washes away the flavour.*

# Octopus salad with potatoes, roast peppers and aioli

### Serves 6–8

1 quantity Cooked Octopus (see recipe page 92)

2–3 waxy potatoes, boiled and cut into ¾ in/2 cm cubes or use small, whole potatoes

12 black olives (good quality)

1 cup roasted bell peppers/capsicums (see recipe below) or 9 oz/250 g cherry tomatoes.

**SIMPLE SALAD DRESSING**

½ cup fresh lemon juice

½ cup extra virgin olive oil

salt and freshly ground black pepper, to taste

**ROASTED OR GRILLED BELL PEPPERS/CAPSICUM**

2–3 bell peppers/capsicums, any colour—a mixture of colours is good, the red bell peppers taste sweeter

**AIOLI**

1 quantity Saffron Mayonnaise (see recipe page 205)

1–2 cloves garlic, minced

Mix the octopus, potatoes, olives and the roasted or grilled bell peppers together.

Dress the salad with the Simple Salad Dressing.

Add the aioli last of all: drizzle half the aioli over the salad (do not mix it in) and present the rest of the aioli (method below) in a bowl so guests can add more if they wish.

## ROASTED OR GRILLED BELL PEPPERS/CAPSICUM

Place the bell peppers on a barbecue grill and cook over intense heat until the skin is charred and puffy. Turn them from time to time to ensure even blistering and charring. As you remove the charred bell peppers from the heat, place them in a bowl covered with a plate or a lid where they will keep on cooking and they will also be easier to peel (leave for at least 10 minutes). Or you can wrap them in paper or put them in a plastic bag, which my mother used to do.

When the bell peppers are ready, peel off the skins and scrape out the seeds. Slice or tear the peppers into rough strips.

## AIOLI

Use the recipe for making Saffron Mayonnaise on page 205. Omit the saffron and replace it with 1–2 cloves of minced garlic. I prefer to use roasted garlic. I usually roast whole heads of garlic when I make a roast and store it in the fridge in jars topped with extra virgin olive oil. Using fresh garlic is the cheat version.

*My sister-in-law makes her version of this salad on Christmas day.*

# Shrimp with cannellini beans

*Serves 6*

Put peeled shrimp in a bowl with half the olive oil, half the lemon juice and lots of freshly ground black pepper. Mix well and set aside for about 30 minutes.

Drain and rinse the cannellini beans. Transfer the beans and the shrimp to a serving bowl and stir in the red onion, preserved lemons, parsley and cherry tomatoes.

To make the dressing, combine the remaining oil and the lemon juice with the crushed garlic and mustard in a screw-topped jar and shake well.

Dress the salad and top with basil and avocado. Mix everything through gently and serve straight away.

36 oz/1 kg cooked shrimp/ prawns, peeled, with the tail left on

6 tablespoons olive oil

lemon juice, from 1-2 lemons

freshly ground black pepper

2 x 14 oz/400 g cans cannellini beans

1 small red onion, quartered and finely sliced

2 preserved lemons, cut finely

2 tablespoons flat-leaf parsley, roughly chopped

5 oz/150 g cherry tomatoes cut in half

1 clove garlic, crushed

1 teaspoon Dijon mustard

handful fresh basil, roughly shredded

2 avocados, peeled, stoned and thinly sliced

*Dried beans are very popular in Italian cooking and I like all types of pulses. I cook my own and always have a container of ready-cooked beans in my freezer.*

*This very simple salad was popular as an antipasto when I was growing up in Trieste. In the Triestian dialect tuna salad with borlotti beans is called* Insalata di tonno, fazoi e zivola; *Trieste is in morth-eastern Italy not far from Venice. If you are ever in Trieste you are likely to still find this salad in any trattoria that has a buffet and also in homes.*

# Tuna salad with borlotti beans

### Serves 6

In a bowl, break the tuna up with a fork and then fold in the borlotti beans and onion rings.

Mix together the olive oil, red wine vinegar and the mustard and stir through the salad—that's it!

Refrigerate at least one hour before serving. Young rocket leaves or red radicchio leaves can be placed underneath the salad, but this is optional.

14 oz/425 g canned tuna in oil, drained
2 cups canned borlotti beans
1 red onion, finely sliced into rings
1 cup extra virgin olive oil
1/3 cup red wine vinegar
1 teaspoon French mustard

# Raw and marinated fish

When lemon juice or vinegar is used to 'cook' fish in Italy, it's referred to as Fish Carpaccio or *Pesce Marinato*. In South America, lime juice is often used and the dish is called *ceviche*.

In both cases, the acid changes the texture of the fish, without altering the taste very much. It is important to use the freshest, cleanest fish possible. Just about any fish or shellfish will do.

For an antipasto, 4 oz/100 g of raw fish per person is usually enough. You may like to partly freeze the fish to make slicing easier.

Fresh bread or any of the crostini (see Crostini and Canapés recipe on page 157) can be used to eat the fish.

Top with fresh herbs if you wish, such as parsley, fennel or mint. Dill or chervil are also good herbs with fish but are not generally used in Italian cooking.

# Fish carpaccio

## Serves 6

Arrange fish slices in a single layer on a large shallow glass or ceramic dish.

Mix the extra virgin olive oil with the lemon juice and a little salt.

Pour the dressing on top about 20 minutes before serving.

Decorate with very thinly cut slices of lemon or capers and sprinkle over some black pepper. For a different taste, try grinding pink peppercorns instead of black pepper. You can use a few fresh herbs on top rather than the lemon slices.

In Middle Eastern cooking (*kibbeh*) and in Japanese cooking (*sushi* and *sashimi*) raw fish is served without marinades. If you wish you could use the marinade as a dipping sauce and serve it separately.

16–24 oz/500–700 g white fish, skinless and boneless, sliced as thinly as possible—wafer-thin
¾ cup extra virgin olive oil
juice of 1 lemon
a little salt
1 lemon, very thinly sliced
½ cup capers
freshly ground black pepper
herbs (optional)

*For this dish, if you don't want to use salmon, any firm, white-fleshed fish is also suitable.*

# Marinated salmon with coconut milk

*Serves 6*

16–24oz/500–700 g salmon, skinned and de-boned, and then cut into small cubes about ½ in/1 cm
½ cup fresh lime juice plus 1 tablespoon extra
1 teaspoon grated palm sugar
½ teaspoon salt
1 cup coconut cream
zest of 1 lime
cilantro/coriander leaves, for garnish
scallions/spring onions, for garnish
chillies, de-seeded, cut into long strips, for garnish

Place the fish in a glass or ceramic shallow dish with the lime juice, sugar and salt. Place in the refrigerator for at least 2 hours (overnight will not spoil it).

Remove fish from dish and drain well.

Mix the coconut cream with the rest of the lime juice.

Arrange the fish on a large plate and spoon the coconut cream and lime juice mixture on top. Decorate if you wish to do so before presenting it to your guests. I quite like to eat it unadorned.

*Two of my friends discovered this recipe on one of their trips to Scandinavia. The hotel they were staying in served this for breakfast. I really like this because it has a dressing, unlike most smoked salmon slices placed on crispbread. I am also rather fond of the idea of having irregularly shaped broken crispbread on the plate. It may sound plain but it can look surreal and tastes pretty good!*

# Smoked salmon on crispbread with a dill sauce

### Serves 6

multi-grain rye crispbread, broken into bite-sized pieces

7 oz/200 g smoked salmon or gravlax

sprigs of dill

very thin slices of lemon

**DILL MUSTARD SAUCE**

½ cup Dijon mustard

1 teaspoon sugar

1 tablespoon plain or white wine vinegar

1 tablespoon canola oil

4 tablespoons roughly chopped dill

To make the sauce, mix the mustard, sugar, vinegar and canola oil until you have a smooth sauce.

Stir in the chopped dill. Keep the sauce chilled until needed. It will keep, covered, in the fridge for a week.

Lay out the crispbread slices, spread each one with dill mustard sauce. Place some smoked salmon on top, then a slice of lemon and a small sprig of dill.

*Sicilians like to eat sardines* crude e condite *(raw and dressed).*
*Sardines are sustainable, and a good choice if you are concerned about the environment. Marinated sardines make*
*a great antipasto and lose that strong fishy taste disliked by those people-who-do-not-like-sardines.*

# Sardines raw and dressed

## Sardine crude e condite
### Serves 4–6

Arrange the fish in one layer on a plate and pour the juice of the lemons on top (this lemon juice will be discarded).

Seal with plastic wrap and refrigerate for 3 to 6 hours. They are ready when they have turned almost white.

Drain the juice from the fish well. I use a colander and then quickly dry the fish on kitchen paper.

Arrange the fillets in a single layer on a large plate.

Sprinkle the fish with herbs, garlic and salt and pepper.

Dress with the extra virgin olive oil, cover with plastic wrap and refrigerate again for about 30 minutes until ready to serve.

This dish would be delicious with an orange salad. Mix together some peeled and skinned oranges, sliced finely and dressed with extra virgin olive oil, salt and pepper, thin rings of red onion, olives and some fresh parsley or mint leaves.

Photos overleaf.

12 sardines (1–3 sardine fillets
  per person)
juice of 3–4 lemons
½ cup finely chopped parsley
  and oregano
2 cloves garlic, minced
salt and freshly ground black
  pepper
extra virgin olive oil

SALAD
2 oranges, peeled and skinned,
  sliced finely
extra virgin olive oil
salt and pepper
1 red onion, peeled and thinly
  sliced into rings
a handful of black olives
fresh parsley or mint leaves,
  to garnish

# Soused fried fish

What I like about soused fish is that it can be made days beforehand—the flavour just improves with time.

My grandmother always soused fish in her kitchen in Sicily. It was a way of preserving food before refrigeration by saturating foods with acid: vinegar in this case.

Soused fish is also found in other parts of Italy and elsewhere—*pesce alla scapace* in central and southern Italy and *escabeche*, often served as tapas, in Spain and Portugal. It is also common in France and North Africa. My German friend puts mustard seeds and dill in his soused fish; others add black peppercorns, bay leaves and coriander seeds.

Oily fish, such as sardines, sprats, kippers, mullet, mackerel, kingfish, bonito, trevally and eel, are good for soused fish. Leave the skin on as it will help to hold the flesh together.

*I lived in Trieste for a time and we mostly ate the Venetian version with sardines, which is called* sarde in saor. *It is often eaten with white polenta (the yellow polenta is usually an accompaniment to meat).*
*You can buy fillets of sardines, but it is easy to clean them by hand. Scale them just by using your thumb. Remove the heads and innards. Open the sardine up and remove the backbone. Run your thumb inside the cavity to clean out the innards. Rinse them or wipe them clean (which I prefer) with some kitchen paper. Try to keep the sardine in one piece (butterflied) rather than two halves.*

# Soused sardines

## Sarde in saor
### Serves 6

Wash, pat dry, then lightly salt and flour the sardines.

In a frying pan, over a high heat, fry the sardines in ¼ cup very hot extra virgin olive oil; drain on kitchen paper.

In a separate pan, cook the onions on moderate heat until soft in a few tablespoons of extra virgin olive oil and salt.

Add the vinegar and let it simmer until the vinegar has evaporated a little. The sauce should be sloppy.

Use a ceramic or glass bowl deep enough to hold the ingredients. Make alternate layers of sardines with the onions, then pine nuts, peppercorns and raisins and the occasional bay leaf. The last layer should be onion.

Cover and leave it in the fridge for at least a day before serving.

Serve with crostini or fresh bread.

12–18 fresh sardines (1–3 sardine fillets per person)
all-purpose/plain flour, to coat the fish
salt, to taste
¼ cup extra virgin olive oil
17½ oz/500 g onions, sliced
extra virgin olive oil, for frying
¾ cup white wine vinegar
2 oz/50 g pine nuts
1 teaspoon whole black peppercorns
2 oz/50 g raisins
2–3 fresh bay leaves

*This recipe is a southern Italian version of soused fish. It can also be made successfully with fresh cilantro/coriander, but the flavours will no longer be Italian, but closer to North African.*
*Each guest may eat one to two pieces of fish, but adjust amounts of ingredients accordingly.*

# Soused fish with vinegar, garlic and mint

## Serves 6

12 pieces of fish (each piece of fish could weigh about 4 oz/100 g)

salt to taste

½ cup extra virgin olive oil

2 onions, very finely sliced

12 garlic cloves, cut into slivers

2 hot chillies, de-seeded, scraped and finely shredded

¾ cup white wine vinegar

1 cup mint leaves, on the stems

fresh mint leaves, to garnish

Lightly salt the fish. In a frying pan over a high heat, fry the fish in ¼ cup very hot olive oil. Once cooked, drain on paper towels and pat dry.

Heat the remaining oil in a separate pan and sauté the onions, garlic, chilli and a little salt until the ingredients are slightly softened.

Add the vinegar and evaporate for a few minutes.

Use a ceramic or glass bowl deep enough to hold the ingredients. Layer the fish with fresh mint leaves and the vinegar pickling mixture. Cool it, cover and leave it in the refrigerator for at least a day before serving.

Remove the old mint leaves and decorate with fresh mint leaves when ready to serve.

*This version is for gluttons, and I love it, but I am not sure that a true Middle Eastern person would use all of these flavours.*

# Escabeche with Middle Eastern Flavours

*Serves 6*

12 pieces of fish (each piece of fish could be about 4 oz/100 g)

salt, to taste

all-purpose/plain flour, to coat (optional)

¼ cup extra virgin olive oil, plus extra for frying

2 onions, very finely sliced

2 garlic cloves, cut into slivers

1 hot chilli, de-seeded, scraped and finely shredded

9 fl oz/250 ml white wine

¾ cup white wine vinegar

¼ cup fresh lemon juice and grated peel of 1 lemon or 1 tablespoon preserved lemon peel, chopped finely

2 teaspoons sumac

2 teaspoons Ras El Hanout (see recipe Baked Scallops with a Multitude of Flavours page 171)

2 pinches saffron

2 carrots, cut into short batons

½ cup parsley or cilantro/ coriander, to garnish

Pat the fish dry, then lightly salt and flour it. Bring the olive oil to a very hot heat in a frying pan and fry the fish in batches. Drain on paper towels.

Heat up the oil again and add the onions. Cook until they are slightly softened. Add the garlic, chilli, white wine and wine vinegar, lemon juice and peel, the spices and carrot. Cook, uncovered, for 2–3 minutes to allow the vinegar and wine to evaporate slightly. Cover and simmer for about 5 minutes.

Layer the fish and the pickling liquid and vegetables into a ceramic or glass bowl deep enough to hold the ingredients. Cool it, cover and leave it in the fridge for at least a day before serving.

Decorate with herbs if you wish (parsley or cilantro) when ready to serve.

# Floured, crumbed & battered

# Frying fish

There are just so many ways that you can coat fish before frying. Select the type of oil you prefer for frying. I like to use extra virgin olive oil for almost everything unless I am preparing something Asian, and then I like to use rice bran oil.

- Dry the fish in paper towels before you dip it into plain flour. Add a little salt. Shake off the excess; too much flour will make the oil cloudy.
- Fry fish a few pieces at the time. If you are concerned about keeping the fish hot (which Italians aren't) use more than one frying pan.
- Cook fish of a similar size and same species together.
- It is a good idea to score the skin of fish (if there is any) to allow the heat to penetrate.
- Use clean, oil in a heavy-based frying pan. Ensure that the oil is hot (340–350°F/170–180°C or smoking) before you add the fish. For shallow frying, have at least ¾ in/2 cm in the bottom of the pan; for deep-frying have 3 in/7 cm.
- As the pieces of fish are cooked, set them on kitchen paper to drain.
- Add more oil to the frying pan as necessary and allow the oil to return to the correct heat before adding the next batch.
- If the fish is in plenty of oil it may not need to be turned, but if you need to turn it, do this only once to stop it breaking.
- The fish will cook very quickly (in a few minutes). To see if it's cooked, poke the tip of a knife into the thickest part of the fish and if the flesh pulls away from the bone, it's ready to be served.
- It is important to remember that the fish, especially if it has been battered, will keep on cooking once removed from the oil.

# Flour coatings

## Flour

plain flour

Place plain flour in a paper bag or a shallow dish. Coat the fish well with the flour, a few pieces at a time, and shake off excess flour.

Fry a few pieces at a time in hot oil in no less than ¼ in/1 cm oil (otherwise the oil could foam).

Fry for 2–3 minutes each side until crisp and golden. Place the fried fish on kitchen paper to drain. Cover with more paper to keep warm if necessary.

## Flour and egg

flour • 1–2 eggs, lightly beaten

Prepare the fish as in the Flour recipe, but, after you have dipped the fish into flour, dip it into an eggwash made from 1–2 eggs that have been lightly beaten with a pinch of salt.

Fry for 2–3 minutes each side until crisp and golden. Place the fried fish on kitchen paper to drain. Cover with more paper to keep warm if necessary.

# Crumb coatings

## Dry fine breadcrumbs

flour • 1–2 eggs, lightly beaten • dry, fine breadcrumbs

Preare the fish as described for flour and egg, dip the fish into an egg wash made from 1–2 eggs that have been lightly beaten with a pinch of salt, then dip it in dry fine breadcrumbs and then in egg mixture once again.

Fry for 2–3 minutes each side until crisp and golden. Place the fried fish on kitchen paper to drain. Cover with more paper to keep warm if necessary.

## Fresh breadcrumbs

Prepare fresh breadcrumbs, made with day-old bread, crusts removed. Prepare the fish in the same way as the dry fine breadcrumbs recipe above using the fresh breadcrumbs.

Fry for 2–3 minutes each side until crisp and golden. Place the fried fish on kitchen paper to drain. Cover with more paper to keep warm if necessary.

## Panko crumbs

These are airy, large flakes that give fried foods a light, crunchy coating. They are popular in Japan. Use like dry fine or fresh breadcrumbs.

Fry for 2–3 minutes each side until crisp and golden. Place the fried fish on kitchen paper to drain. Cover with more paper to keep warm if necessary.

## Polenta

Use polenta the same as you would in the dry fine or fresh breadcrumbs, but, after you have dipped the fish into an eggwash of lightly beaten eggs with a pinch of salt, dip into fine polenta. Semolina also works. It can be dry, but it adds a little bit of crunch.

Fry for 2–3 minutes each side until crisp and golden. Place the fried fish on kitchen paper to drain. Cover with more paper to keep warm if necessary.

# Batters

## Rich egg batter

5 oz/150 g (about 1 cup) all-purpose/plain flour, mixed with a little salt  •  2 eggs  •  2 egg yolks
•  1½ cups water (sparkling water is preferable)

Lightly beat eggs and yolks with water and add to dry ingredients. Mix or beat the batter until smooth. Add more water if necessary; the batter will have the consistency of a pancake batter. Rest for one hour in the refrigerator before use.

Deep-frying the fish. Lightly dust the fish in some flour, immediately dip in the batter, shake off the excess and submerge in hot oil. Turn pieces occasionally so they don't stick.

## Saffron batter

Prepare as for the rich egg batter above, but add some saffron that has been infused in a little warm water to the batter mixture. Deep-frying is preferable.

## Simple beer batter

5 oz/150 g all-purpose/plain flour (1 cup) or a mixture of self-raising and all-purpose/plain flour  •  1 cup beer or water
(or a mix of the two)  •  2 egg whites, beaten until stiff  •  a little salt

Mix together the flour(s) with the beer, then fold in the egg whites. Mix lightly.
Deep-frying is preferable. Fry as in the Rich Egg Batter recipe above.

## Tempura batter

2 egg yolks  •  3½ oz/100 g cornstarch/cornflour  •  7 fl oz/200 ml ice-cold water, preferably soda or sparkling (you
may need a little more than this, depending on the batter)  •  extra cornstarch/flour, for dusting  •  oil, for frying

Use chilled ingredients. In a mixing bowl, add the egg yolks and iced water together and mix very lightly. Do not beat. Add flour all at once and mix very lightly (I use chopsticks). The mixture will be slightly lumpy. Use batter immediately.

Deep-frying is preferable for this. Fry as in the Rich Egg Batter recipe above.

*This is a Greek favourite and is eaten with skordalia. Either buy pre-soaked cod or follow instructions for soaking as in the recipe for Salt cod fritters with green olive paste or saffron mayonnaise (see recipe page 204). The bakaliaros (Greek) is just dipped lightly in flour and fried, and Sicilians and Spaniards seem to cook it in the same way. I have eaten it in Spain with Romesco sauce (see recipe on page 125) and the fish was sprinkled with pimenton.*

# Salt cod with skordalia

## Baccalà with skordalia
### Serves 6

Skin and bone the cod and cut into bite-sized pieces or into a slice. (As with any fish, if you want the fish to curl, leave the skin on.)

Combine flour with salt and pepper and coat the fish with the flour, shaking off any excess.

Heat the oil over high heat and gently cook the fish in batches. The fish needs to cook very quickly to keep it crisp and golden.

Drain the cooked fish on kitchen paper.

This dish is commonly served plain with lemon wedges or a little fresh parsley. If you wish, present it with a dollop of skordalia (see recipe on page 124). Black olives or some Romesco sauce will add colour.

1 lb 9oz/700 g dried salt cod (baccalà or bacalao or bakaliaros), soaked beforehand
1 cup all-purpose/plain flour
pinch of salt and black pepper
extra virgin olive oil, for frying
lemon wedges, to serve
parsley, whole sprigs with tough stems removed, to decorate
Skordalia (see recipe page 124) (optional)
black olives, to serve (optional)
Romesco Sauce (see Battered Fish (and Scallops) with Romesco Sauce page 125)

*Use a mortar and pestle to make this as a food processor is not suitable for creaming potato. The mortar and pestle has been used since antiquity and is still widely used in Sicily. It is very different in function from a blender or food processor—the textures and consistencies obtained from these utensils will be very different. The ingredients are added gradually to achieve the texture of a smooth purée. As a variation, I add some blanched ground almonds and this not only adds taste, but also texture. Hot water is added during the mashing to make the mixture smoother. I also know that in various parts of Greece, walnuts are used and that sometimes skordalia is made with white bread (soaked in water and squeezed) instead of potatoes.*

# Skordalia

*Makes about 17½ fl oz/500 ml*

2–3 cloves garlic
salt to taste
¼ cup blanched and ground
   almonds (toasted is optional)
14 oz/400 g potatoes, cooked,
   peeled and cubed
½–¾ cup extra virgin olive oil
juice of 1 lemon
hot water

Begin by pounding the garlic and salt in the mortar and pestle.
   Gradually add small amounts of almonds, potato and some of the oil, some of the lemon juice and continue to pound until all of the ingredients have been added and you have a smooth paste. Taste and adjust seasoning. You will need to add some hot water during this process to thin the sauce as you pound it.
   The mixture should resemble creamy mashed potato.

*There are just so many ways to make batter, but for fish and chips I like a simple beer batter (see recipe page 121). There are so many variations to making Romesco sauce, a Catalan condiment, but the most common ingredients seem to be garlic, red bell peppers/capsicums, tomatoes, white bread and almonds. Because my grandmothers were Sicilian and this is a Catalan recipe I cannot say that this is how it is made in my family. However, I can give you what works for me. There is always room for improvement and I will keep on experimenting.*

# Battered fish (and scallops) with romesco sauce

## Serves 6

Sprinkle the fish or scallops with a little salt; dip in the beer batter, drain quickly and fry in hot oil for a few minutes until golden brown. Scallops may take less time to cook.

Serve with hot chips (if you wish) and a small jug of vinegar or old-fashioned tartare sauce (see Vintage Shrimp Balls with Old-fashioned Tartare Sauce on page 201). Or you may wish to present your guests with a little Romesco sauce instead.

## ROMESCO SAUCE

Roast or char-grill the bell peppers whole. If you are roasting or char-grilling the bell peppers, roast the tomatoes whole at the same time. Peel them and remove the seeds and break them into strips (see recipe for Octopus Salad with Potatoes, Roast Peppers and Aioli on page 98).

Heat ¼ cup olive oil in a non-stick frypan and sauté the bread until golden. Set aside.

Sauté the peeled cloves of garlic in the same frying pan. Set aside. Toast the blanched almonds or sauté them in the same frying pan.

Blitz the bread and almonds in a blender. Add the rest of the ingredients plus the rest of the olive oil and blend until it forms a thick, smooth sauce. If the sauce is too thick, add a little water to thin it down.

6 fillets fish, cut into bite-sized pieces (1½ x ½ in/4 x 1.5 cm thick), no bone
6–24 scallops (optional)
salt
Simple Beer Batter (see recipe page 121)
extra virgin olive oil

ROMESCO SAUCE
2 large red bell peppers/capsicums
2 medium-sized ripe tomatoes, roughly chopped
¼ cup extra virgin olive oil plus an extra ½ cup
1 slice stale sourdough bread, cut into small squares
4–5 cloves garlic
½ cup blanched almonds
1 teaspoon pimenton (preferred) or sweet paprika
2 tablespoons sherry vinegar or red wine vinegar
salt to taste

*Use chilli flakes or a little chilli sauce if you do not have* sambal olek *but the taste will be less complex. Guests with easily eat three prawns each, so adjust accordingly.*

# Shrimp in coconut batter with mango salsa

### Serves 6

18 large green king shrimps/
  prawns, peeled, deveined, with
  tails intact
2 cups shredded coconut
2 cups vegetable oil

BATTER
1 tablespoon cilantro/coriander,
  finely chopped
1 cup all-purpose/plain flour
1 cup cornstarch/cornflour
2 teaspoons sambal olek
soda water, enough to give the
  batter the consistency of
  pouring cream

MANGO SALSA
1½ cups mango, finely chopped
  (I prefer this to pureed mango)
½ teaspoon lemon rind, grated
1 tablespoon lemon juice
2 tablespoons finely chopped
  mint or coriander
dash of sweet chilli sauce or
  1 sliced red chilli (optional)

To make the batter, combine all the ingredients in a bowl and whisk gently until the batter has the required consistency.

Either dip each prawn in extra flour then coat in batter separately or thread three shrimp onto a skewer (tail first) and dip each skewer into the flour and then batter.

Roll each shrimp or the skewers in coconut.

Heat the oil in a wok or deep-fryer, and fry the shrimp gently until cooked, about 3–5 minutes.

Serve with the Mango Salsa.

MANGO SALSA
To make Mango Salsa, mix all the dressing ingredients together and serve.

*Although crispy fried whitebait is popular in many countries in the Mediterranean, my fondest memories are of eating them in Greece while drinking ouzo or retsina. In Trieste, we had a next-door neighbour who used to call whitebait rivolta barche which means 'capsize boats', an inverse joke on the size of these fish!*

*For those who have never eaten them, whitebait are tiny, translucent fish; the original small fry which are perfect to do just that—deep-fry and eat whole, heads and all.*

# Fried whitebait

## Serves 6

Combine the flour with the salt and pepper and dredge the fish through the flour, shaking off any excess.

Heat the oil over high heat and gently cook the fish in batches. The whitebait needs to cook very quickly to be crisp and golden.

Remove the whitebait with a slotted spoon and drain on kitchen paper. Repeat with remaining fish.

Pile the hot, fried fish on a plate and sprinkle with more freshly ground black pepper. Serve immediately with lemon wedges. Invite your guests to help themselves.

You can also make fans with the whitebait: hold three whitebaits together by the tail, dip them in flour and then fry them. They stay together and make little fans. I rather like whitebait fans as an alternative serving style.

1 cup all-purpose/plain flour
a little salt and black pepper
17½ oz/500 g whitebait
enough extra virgin olive oil to
 fry them
lemon wedges

*For this recipe you need large, fresh leaves of sage. Within each set of leaves there will be some minced anchovy.*
*These little packages are then dipped in batter and deep-fried. This dish originates from Tuscany.*
*I have assumed that six guests will eat two each. They may want more, but the first time you make them you may find the process fiddly.*
*The mashed anchovies help to hold the sage leaves together.*

# Fried sage leaves stuffed with anchovies

## Fritelle di salvia e acciughe
### Serves 6

Place the flour into a bowl. Make a hole in the centre, break in the egg and slowly add the oil and wine to make a smooth batter. If it looks too thick add a little cold water to get a batter the density of a thick cream. Rest it for about 1 hour.

Wash the sage leaves and place them on kitchen paper to dry. Spread them out so that pairs are roughly the same size and align with each other.

On one sage leaf of each pair place some minced anchovy. Cover with the other leaf and secure each pair with a toothpick threaded vertically, with the longer end following the line of the stems of the pair of leaves. It will hold the contents together.

Dip each pair into the batter very carefully, holding them with the toothpick.

Heat plenty of oil and fry the leaves in hot oil until they are golden. Being so small they cook almost instantly.

Lift them out carefully—you may need to use a slotted spoon or strainer.

Drain them on kitchen paper.

Serve them warm to hot. Sprinkle them with some freshly ground black pepper. Guests can pick them up by the toothpicks.

**BATTER**

5 oz/150 g flour

1 egg

1 tablespoon extra virgin olive oil

3 tablespoons white wine

some cold sparkling water

24 fresh sage leaves, roughly the same size, with stems

6–12 anchovy fillets packed under oil, drained and cut into very small pieces (minced)

½–1 cup extra virgin olive oil, for frying

*The greater the range of seafood and fish you use in this dish, the more visual the impact, but you can also use just one type of fish, for example, shrimp/prawns or calamari, it just will not be a fritto misto (as misto means mixed). Italians just dip the fish into a little plain flour and salt before frying.*

# A plate of mixed fried fish with Italian tartare sauce
## Fritto misto di pesce
### Serves 6–8

Combine any mixture of the following seafood: either 28–35 oz/800 g to 1 kg of mixed seafood—whole small fish and some fish fillets cut into bite-sized pieces, whole green shrimp/prawns (with tails, with or without shells), rings or strips of calamari scored with cuts (use a serrated knife)—or buy single units of seafood, for example: 6-8 prawns, 6-8 scallops, etc.

## ITALIAN TARTARE SAUCE
4 hard-boiled eggs, yolks removed
extra virgin olive oil
1 cup Mayonnaise (see recipe page 91)
1 tablespoon capers
3-4 cetriolini (small pickled gherkins, not sweet), thinly sliced
1 teaspoon finely chopped parsley
1 teaspoon finely chopped tarragon

Dry the fish on kitchen paper before you dip it into plain flour with a little salt added. Shake off the excess flour.

Heat some oil in a frying pan and, once it is hot, fry fish a few at the time.

Cook fish of the same species and of similar size together. Follow the instructions for frying fish in the Floured, Crumbed and Battered chapter.

Vegetables can also be added to a fritto misto, if you wish. Fry the fish and the vegetables separately in new oil. Try carrots and zucchini/courgette cut into batons, large whole sage leaves (with stems) and zucchini/courgette flowers. These will fry better if dipped in batter (use either a tempura batter or egg batter—see Batter recipes on page 121). Use fresh oil when you fry the vegetables. You could use two pans and fry the vegetables in a separate pan while you fry the fish at the same time. Follow the same procedures as for frying fish.

The fish is usually presented warm with lemon wedges and Italian tartare sauce.

To make the tartare sauce, in a bowl, grind the yolks of the eggs into a smooth paste using the back of a spoon. Add in a little oil. Add in the egg mayonnaise, cetriolini and herbs.

Note: Italians call tarragon *dragoncello*, meaning 'little dragon'.

*People seem to find the combination of salt and pepper squid irresistible.*
*Salt and pepper squid can be ordered almost anywhere in various disguises, dipped in flour or a light batter, as long as it's fried. A dry batter seems to be the most preferred method (see below). For variations use a Tempura Batter (see recipe page 134) or just roll them in cornstarch/cornflour. I toast all my spices in an old cast iron frying pan.*

# Salt and pepper squid

## Serves 6

2 teaspoons salt (I like flakes)
3 teaspoons Szechuan and white peppercorns (according to taste) or pink peppercorns (strictly not traditional)
24 oz/700 g fresh squid
cilantro/coriander leaves, for garnish

### BATTER
1 tablespoon vegetable oil
2 tablespoons self-rising/self-raising flour
a little cornstarch/cornflour
pinch of salt
vegetable oil, for deep-frying

Use medium-low to medium heat and toast the salt and peppercorns. Stir until the peppercorns are fragrant (the salt may start to turn a light brown colour).

Remove from the heat. Cool, then grind and set aside.

Use rings, tentacles or triangles of fresh cleaned squid. Dry on paper towels before dipping into batter. If using strips or triangles of squid, use a serrated knife to score the flesh in a criss-cross fashion. Use the tentacles as well.

In a bowl, mix the oil and a little water with self-rising flour to make a paste.

Dip the squid pieces into the batter, then dip each one into a little cornflour. Shake off excess and fry in abundant oil until golden.

Serve garnished with some cilantro leaves, with the salt and pepper mix on the side for dipping.

### VARIATION
Rather than using battered fish, you could also use the salt and pepper mixture with grilled squid.

*For grilled squid, I have to admit that I prefer a salmorigano dressing, which is a Sicilian dressing, a legacy from the Greeks. The Spanish-speaking countries would probably use a chermoula dressing. Alternatively, use one of the Asian dipping sauces (see Rice Paper Rolls with Dipping Sauces page 70).*

# simple grilled squid

## Serves 6

You can grill the cleaned squid whole or use large pieces of cleaned, scored squid and tentacles. You can cut these into smaller bits if you wish once the squid is cooked.

Brush with a little extra virgin olive oil. Grill the scored side first, 2–3 minutes, turn over and grill some more.

You could serve this with the salt and pepper mixture from the Salt and Pepper Squid recipe (see page 134).

For grilled squid, I have to admit that I prefer my squid grilled over charcoal with a *Salmorigano* Dressing, which is a Sicilian dressing, a legacy from the Greeks. Mix all the dressing ingredients together. Season the squid with salt and pepper before you grill it and once it is cooked pour the dressing over the squid and serve.

For the *Chermoula* Dressing, mix all of the dressing ingredients together and serve over the cooked squid.

24 oz/700 g squid

**SALMORIGANO DRESSING**
pinch of salt
½ cup extra virgin olive oil
½ teaspoon dried oregano
juice of 1 lemon

**CHERMOULA DRESSING**
1 clove garlic
½ cup finely chopped cilantro/
  coriander
½ cup extra virgin olive oil
2 tablespoons lemon or wine
  vinegar
salt and pepper or chilli flakes,
  to taste
1 teaspoon ground coriander
  seeds
1 teaspoon ground cumin seeds

sozzled

*My mother did a lot of cooking in the late 1960s and early 1970s using cognac to deglaze the pan rather than using wine.*

# Shrimp with cognac

## Gamberi al cognac
### Serves 6

12–18 green shrimp/prawns (I use shelled, cleaned, tails left on)
2 tablespoons extra virgin olive oil
½ cup parsley, finely chopped
2 cloves of garlic, finely chopped
salt (to taste) and plenty of ground black pepper
zest and juice of 1 lemon
¼ cup brandy (or cognac)
2 tablespoons butter

Dry the shrimp on kitchen paper.

Using a large frying pan, sauté the shrimp for 3 minutes in the extra virgin olive oil. Add the parsley and garlic, salt, black pepper and the lemon zest, and continue to cook for a couple more minutes.

Add the brandy and let it evaporate over high heat.

Add the butter and, after it has melted, add lemon juice and serve.

*I love the way we pass on recipes to others. There are so many recipes for making smoked trout pâté and most of them contain the same ingredients: butter, Tabasco sauce, horseradish and mayonnaise. But a friend of mine sent me this one and it contains whisky. His mother-in-law only sent him the list of ingredients from Rosalie Gow's* Cooking with Scotch Whisky. *As for the process, she assumed he would know how to combine all of these ingredients. This is how I am proposing you make it. When I make this pâté I sometimes put it in small glass jars. They look impressive. I know they sometimes use kippers blended with butter and whisky in Scotland, which would be a variation on this theme.*

# Smoked trout pâté with whisky

## *Serves 6*

Combine everything together with the butter except for the trout. Beat until creamy and smooth.

Shred the trout roughly and mix it through the butter mixture. I use my fingers at this stage. Press the mixture into a buttered ramekin or small pot.

Heat a little more butter very gently and, while it is still liquid but has cooled, pour it over the pâté to seal it. Sprinkle with black pepper. Chill until ready to serve.

Before serving, let stand at room temperature for a least 15 minutes to soften and become easily spreadable.

4 oz/100 g softened butter plus extra for sealing
juice of 1 lemon
16 drops Tabasco sauce
ground black pepper
2 tablespoons thick mayonnaise
4 teaspoons raw horseradish (not 'cream')
4 tablespoons whisky
1 large (17½ oz/500 g) smoked trout, skinned and boned

*I particularly like the taste of aniseed and use a lot of fennel in my cooking—fresh and the seeds—and, if I can get it, wild fennel. I also use wine in my cooking and sometimes, to accentuate the taste of the fennel, I use anise-flavoured liqueurs, like Ricard or Pernod, Greek Ouzo or Italian Sambuca. Use any one of these fennel-flavoured, alcoholic drinks in this recipe.*

*In restaurants on the Italian the coast in summer, you will often see* piattoni *(large platters) of mussels presented as a starter to a meal. These are a great favourite. I enjoy setting a large platter of mussels in the centre of the table and inviting guests to help themselves.*

# Mussels with anise-flavoured alcohol

## Serves 6

Sauté the garlic lightly in hot extra virgin olive oil. Use a saucepan that will contain the mussels comfortably.

Add the mussels and toss them around for a couple of minutes.

Add the anise-flavoured alcohol, pepper and the parsley. Cover with a lid and cook until the mussels open.

Remove the mussels and place into another warm saucepan with a lid to keep them hot. If you do not mind presenting the mussels warm, place the opened mussels on a platter (Italians do not seem to bother about keeping food hot).

Evaporate the juices until you have about 1 cup of concentrated liquid. Add lemon juice and pour the juice over the mussels and serve.

Serve with slices of crusty bread, if you like, and use it to soak up the juices.

3–4 cloves garlic, finely chopped
¼ cup extra virgin olive oil
36 oz/1 kg mussels, scrubbed and cleaned of beards
½ cup anise-flavoured alcohol
black pepper, finely ground
1 small bunch flat-leaf parsley, finely chopped
juice of 1–2 lemons (grated peel optional as a garnish)
crusty bread loaf, sliced, to serve (optional)

# Oyster shooters

I am a latecomer to oyster shooters, preferring to slip down a raw oyster and follow it with the liquid refreshment—a shot of ice-cold vodka, a margarita or a sparkling white wine. Friends gave me some of these recipes and now I am converted. These should keep your guests entertained.

All of these recipes serve 12 (or less if your guests really love oysters).

# Oysters with vodka or tequila

Place an oyster, with its juice, into a small shot glass, add a few pepper flakes. Top with a shot of ice-cold vodka or tequila.

Add a squeeze of lemon juice and serve.

12 freshly shucked, raw oysters, chilled

a pinch of red pepper flakes (to taste)

shot of ice-cold vodka or tequila

lemon juice, to serve

# Bloody Mary oyster shooters

The beauty of this one is that you can omit the vodka for those friends who do not drink alcohol.

Combine the tomato juice, vodka and Worcestershire sauce in a jug. Add Tabasco sauce to taste and season with salt and pepper. Cover and chill until very cold.

To serve, place an oyster in each glass and pour over the Bloody Mary mixture.

Garnish with a small stick of celery—I like it sticking out of the glass, leaves up.

12 freshly shucked, raw oyster, chilled

12 shot glasses, chilled

12 tender, inner stalks of celery

DRESSING

1 cup tomato juice

¼ cup vodka or to taste

2 teaspoons Worcestershire sauce

Tabasco sauce, to taste

Sea salt and freshly ground pepper

# Oysters with cointreau and lime juice

Place an oyster with its juice into a small shot glass.
Top with a shot of ice-cold Cointreau.
Add a squeeze of lime juice in each glass and serve.

12 freshly shucked, raw oysters, chilled
shot of Cointreau
lime juice, to serve

# Oysters with champagne and scallion dressing

Use a champagne or sparkling white wine that you would serve to guests, as only a small amount is needed for the dressing and a glass of the very same cold bubbly is the perfect accompaniment.

You can use Chinese soup spoons to serve these if you wish.

Combine the dressing ingredients in a bowl and season. Make sure that you work with cold ingredients or place in the fridge until you are ready to use.

Place an oyster in each spoon (or leave it in its shell) and spoon on the dressing carefully. Make sure each oyster gets some of the scallion and cucumber.

Serve immediately.

12 freshly shucked, raw oysters, chilled

DRESSING
1 tablespoon champagne, sherry or wine vinegar
4 tablespoons champagne or your chilled sparkling wine
1 tablespoon very finely diced scallion/spring onion
1 tablespoon very finely diced cucumber
salt and freshly ground pepper

# Spreads

*Some of you may remember fish paste from years ago. It was sold in small jars and could be bought in grocery stores. I thought it tasted medicinal. My English mother-in-law often talked about proper fish paste made with anchovies — simple stuff, and much better tasting than the storebought version. It makes a tasty spread on crostini (see recipe Crostini and canapés page 157). Another friend told me about her mother's love of this paste and her mother would cut the bread with a biscuit cutter in the shape of a fish. Use fewer anchovies if you are not a lover of anchovies.*

# Anchovy butter

*Serves 6*

9 oz/150–250 g anchovy fillets, chopped finely

7 oz/200 g butter

2 garlic cloves

juice of ½ lemon

pinch each of ground cinnamon, mace or nutmeg, ground black pepper

1 tablespoon butter, melted, to cover

Use a food processor to blend the anchovies and butter together, then add all the other ingredients. I like using a spoon to blend the remaining ingredients, except for the melted butter, together.

Spoon the paste into a small container and cover with a little melted butter and chill before serving.

Before serving, let the butter stsand at room temperature for at least 15 minutes to soften and become easily spreadable. If you wish, you can also whip the mixture with a fork before serving.

*Having lived in Trieste (north Italy), I am particularly fond of* baccalà mantecato *(boiled salt cod, whipped or beaten with oil and garlic). This is one of the most representative recipes of Venetian cuisine. Do not be put off by the amount of oil it needs!*

*This spread has the thickness of a creamy, mashed potato. The fish is served cold and when I ate it as a child we always spread it on crostini — either thin slices of white bread, lightly fried until crisp in extra virgin olive oil or just plain crostini (see recipe Crostini and canapés page 157) The baccalà mantecato is usually presented shaped into a mound and passed around to guests while they drink a vermouth as an* aperitivo.

# Salt cod beaten to a cream

## Baccalà mantecato
### Serves 6

21 oz/600 g salted codfish (pre-soaked, see Salt Cod Fritters with Green Olive Paste or Saffron Mayonnaise page 204)

36 fl oz/1 litre water

36 fl oz/1 litre milk

2-3 bay leaves

1 clove garlic, minced

½ cup–¾ cup extra virgin olive oil,

1-2 tablespoons parsley, finely chopped

freshly ground black pepper

Cover the pre-soaked codfish with cold water and milk. Add more liquid if the baccalà is not submerged. Boiling the codfish in a mixture of milk and water helps to keep it white.

Add the bay leaves and bring the liquid slowly to the boil. Take it off the heat and let it rest.

Allow it to cool in the liquid and leave it in the liquid until you are ready to use it. It will take 20–30 minutes to cool (you should be able to flake the fish).

Remove the fish from the poaching liquid, pick out all the bones and discard the skin. Use a fork to break the flesh into small pieces. A narrow bowl is best if you are not using a food processor.

Place the fish and garlic in a bowl and add about ½ cup of extra virgin olive oil. Begin to beat the fish with a wooden spoon and keep on adding oil as you would if you were making mayonnaise by hand. The mixture will look like a thick fluffy cream. You can use a food processor if you pulse the mixture instead of blending continuously, which will make the mixture far too smooth.

Keep on adding oil until the mixture will not absorb any more. Add in the parsley. Shape into a mountain and grind some black pepper on top. Serve with bread crostini (see recipe page 157).

*My friend, who lives very close to a beach, is always entertaining guests. I imagine famished guests hopping into these after some activity in or out of the water.*

# Crabmeat and feta spread on toasted bread

*Serves 6*

**RED PEPPER GARNISH**
2 red bell peppers/capsicums
2 tablespoons olive oil
a little salt and pepper

**SPREAD**
7 oz/200 g soft feta, such as
    Danish feta
¼ cup lemon juice
2 tablespoons extra virgin olive
    oil
6 oz/180 g crab meat, either
    fresh or frozen (thawed), finely
    shredded
2 scallions/spring onions, thinly
    sliced
2 tablespoons basil, finely
    shredded
2 tablespoons finely chopped
    flat-leaf parsley
baguette, to serve

Make the red pepper garnish beforehand. Place the peppers in a ceramic ovenproof baking dish, drizzle with olive oil and roast at 350°F/180°C for 30–40 minutes, or until starting to brown. When cool, clean and de-seed and cut into julienne strips.

For an alternative method of cooking peppers, I use the barbecue (see recipe Octopus Salad with Potatoes, Roast Peppers and Aioli on page 98).

Combine the drained feta, lemon juice and olive oil in a large bowl and mix with a fork until smooth. Season to taste.

Add the crabmeat, onions and herbs, and mix until combined. Refrigerate until ready to use.

Serve on slices of good-quality baguette, toasted if you wish.

Spread feta and crab mixture on slices of bread and garnish with roasted pepper strips and extra basil or parsley if you wish.

*Crostini are small pieces of toasted, grilled or fried bread served with a topping as a starter or canapé. Nothing magical—making crostini is simple. Crostini can be made out of different types of bread. They can be baked or fried. Use slices of bread cut into the shapes you want: the easiest are squares or rectangles, or use fancy biscuit cutters or scone cutters to cut rounds. Cut the bread diagonally for a greater surface area.*

# Crostini and canapés

bread, cut into ½ in/2 cm slices • butter or oil

Preheat the oven to 430°F/220°C. Brush both sides of the bread with extra virgin olive oil.

Arrange the slices on large baking sheets/trays lined with baking parchment/paper. Bake until the tops are golden, about 5–10 minutes. Rotate the sheets and turn crostini over once during baking. Cool before using.

Alternatively, omit brushing the bread with oil and just bake the cut bread following the same procedure above, but bake at 400°F/200°C. Cool before using.

GARLIC BREAD • extra virgin olive oil • butter • minced garlic • bread, cut into ½ in/2 cm slices

In a small saucepan, combine some extra virgin olive oil, butter and minced garlic. When it has melted, remove from heat and brush both sides of the bread with this mixture. Proceed to bake the sliced bread as described above. Use hot or cold.

FRIED CROSTINI • bread, cut into ½ in/2 cm slices • olive oil

Heat some olive oil over medium-high heat in a non-stick frypan (containing about ¼ in/½ cm of oil). Do not crowd the bread in the pan and turn only once. Fry until golden. Add more oil as you fry the rest of the slices. Drain on kitchen paper. Use hot or cold.

BRUSCHETTA • bread, cut into 2 in/5 cm slices • 1–2 garlic cloves, sliced in half • extra virgin olive oil

Grill the slices of cut bread over moderate heat on a barbecue. While they're still hot, rub them gently with the cut side of a garlic clove and drizzle with good-quality extra virgin olive oil. Serve the bruschetta while it is still warm.

*I like to make and serve my potted shrimp in small preserving jars. It is not an original idea but for me it brings back memories of a very special wine bar in Paris, where terrines, mousses and potted fish were all presented in small, commercial glass jars. The pots were placed on a wooden board with a small loaf of bread, a bread knife and a small knife to take out the potted prawns and spread them on the bread. It was meant to be a homely touch — a calculated effect and very impressive. I have also used a mixture of shrimp/prawns and crabmeat. Some of the mixture can also be replaced with cooked, white, shredded fish or salmon.*

# potted shrimp

*Makes about 17½ oz/500 g*

9 oz/250 g unsalted butter

3–4 fresh bay leaves

1 pinch nutmeg

17 ½ oz/500 g cooked shrimp/ prawns cut into small pieces or 9 oz/250g cooked, shredded crabmeat and 9 oz/250 g shrimp/prawns

2 teaspoons finely chopped dill or French tarragon

zest of 1 lemon, finely grated

black pepper, coarsely ground or pink peppercorns

salt to taste

rye or crusty white bread

Gently melt the butter in a shallow saucepan, add the bay leaves and nutmeg. Cook gently for less than a minute.

Pour the butter into a jug and leave about 15 minutes. The milky solids may settle to the bottom. Remove the bay leaves and use again later (or use fresh ones).

Mix together the shrimp (or shrimp and shredded crab), dill or tarragon and lemon zest, and add the freshly ground pepper.

Add a pinch of salt and 2–3 tablespoons of the clarified butter. Mix gently.

Place a little of the clear (clarified) butter in the bottom of your jars or bowls (taking care to leave behind the milky solids in the bottom of the jug if there are any).

Fill the jars with the mixture and press it down really well with the back of a spoon. If you're using glass jars some of the bay leaves can be placed on the side of the glass to show through.

Smooth the surface of the mixture and pour over the clarified butter to completely cover and seal it. Cool and cover each pot with plastic wrap and refrigerate until ready for use.

Remove the potted shrimp from the fridge 20 minutes before you want to serve them or until the butter is soft and spreadable.

You may wish to compare this to the recipe for potted shrimp that is in a book called *Cre-Fydd's Family Fare: The Young Housewife's Daily Assistant on All Matters Relating to Cookery and Housekeeping* It was published in London in 1864.

As my friend The Old Foodie (who has a copy of this book) tells me, the name, or word 'Cre-Fydd' is a mystery to her. It appears to be a pseudonym, but she has not been able to find out the real name of the author.

## POTTED SHRIMPS

Take off the shells of two quarts of fresh-boiled shrimps; season with the sixth part of a nutmeg, grated, two grains of cayenne, a salt spoonful of white pepper, and a quarter of a pound of fresh butter, dissolved.

Press the shrimps into pots or a small pie-dish; pour over the top two ounces of dissolved butter. When firm they are fit for use. Another way, and sometimes preferred, is to pound the shrimps to a paste, add the seasoning, and finish as directed.

*There is nothing like the complex flavours of good-quality smoked fish. Oily fish are particularly great for smoking and eel is the oiliest of them all. Other oily fish are mackerel, salmon, herring and trout. Although these recipes are for eel, use any of the fish above, but the flavour of eel is more intense and so a little eel goes a long way. I buy smoked eel, vacuum-packed. The easiest way to present it is to peel the skin back and present it with fresh bread, biscuits or crostini. I use pumpernickel or rye crispbread. Add a small dollop of grated horseradish (either bought in a jar or mix fresh grated horseradish with a little sour cream). Alternatively, eat it as a pâté.*

# smoked eel pâté

### Serves 6

Mix the eel with the butter, horseradish and a little of the lemon zest. I use my fingers to do this. You can decorate the pâté with the herbs or add 1 tablespoon of finely chopped herbs to the mixture.

Press the mixture into a buttered ramekin or small pot. Place a few whole leaves of the herb you have used on top.

Heat a little more butter very gently and, while it is still liquid but has cooled, pour it over the pâté to seal it. Sprinkle with black pepper. Chill until ready to serve.

Before serving, let stand at room temperature for at least 15 minutes to soften and become easily spreadable.

1 cup smoked eel, flaked (or smoked fish)
3 tablespoons softened, unsalted butter
a little grated horseradish (or prepared horseradish)
a little grated lemon zest
herbs, such as fennel, dill or tarragon, finely chopped
whole leaves of the herbs used, to garnish
extra butter, melted, to cover

*This recipe was given to me by an elderly woman and I particularly like the way the bread is cut in the shape of a fish with a biscuit cutter. Perhaps it was so when you had mixed canapés you knew which were the fishy ones. There are many brands of very good quality sardines packed in olive oil. The decoration is optional, but could be quite fun to do.*

# Retro fish-shaped savouries topped with mashed sardines

Preheat the oven to 400°F/200°C. Butter white sliced bread, then cut fish shapes into it with a small cookie cutter.

Bake the bread in the oven until crisp and golden. Cool before using.

Mash the sardines or cut the drained roll mops into edible bits (to fit on the bread).

Season to taste and add a squeeze of lemon.

When ready to serve, spread the mixture on toasted fish shapes and put on pepper.

Decorate sardine paste with a small cocktail onion or if using the roll mops, decorate with a sliced small cornichon.

Arrange on a platter and serve cold with drinks.

Crème de menthe or perhaps a sweet sherry will carry through the retro theme.

I loved the idea of using a canapé in the shape of a fish so much, that I tried them with some of my marinated white anchovies (see recipe Zucchini and Mint Fritters with Marinated White Anchovies page 192).

white sliced bread
butter
4 oz/120 g tinned sardines or roll
    mops cracked black pepper
juice of 1 lemon
small cocktail onions or small
    cornichons, to decorate
cracked black pepper, to taste

Hefty shells

# Cockles (also called vongole, pipis or clams)

When I first left Italy, I found that in many places, cockles, like squid, were not considered food and were used as bait. How strange my family must have seemed collecting cockles from the beaches. We weren't alone, collecting cockles was a favourite activity for other Southern European families as well.

Little did the locals looking on know that we were going home to eat them with spaghetti (*pasta alle vongole*) or in a risotto. We also steamed them and ate them with a soffritto (see recipe Vongole with soffritto on page 174 ) and sometimes we even ate them raw with a squeeze of lemon juice, just like oysters.

There are now Government restrictions for the amount of cockles that can be collected by recreational fishers and commercial fishers. Mechanical harvesting is also restricted and there are open and closed seasons to allow some of the stocks to recuperate.

In Italian, scallops are called capesante (sante *means holy*) and in French they are known as coquilles Saint-Jacques.

This is a very simple, standard recipe for such a blessed fish. There are many combinations of ingredients and herbs and spices that can be used to vary the taste. Use any of the variations below. The simplest recipe for baked scallops is to use dry breadcrumbs, which form a crust. Or you can omit the breadcrumbs and serve the scallops with fresh bread—there will be juices to mop up.

# Baked scallops with a multitude of flavours

Preheat the oven to 430°F/220°C.

Mix the other ingredients together, except the breadcrumbs, and distribute the mixture between the scallops. Top with oiled or buttered breadcrumbs.

Place the scallops on baking sheets/trays to prevent spillage. Bake for 8 minutes or until the breadcrumbs look golden.

## VARIATIONS

Fry six slices of thinly sliced chorizo, pancetta or prosciutto in a little oil until it's crispy. Crumble over the scallops once they have been cooked.

Try adding a little preserved lemon skin to the stuffing mixture. If doing this, omit the lemon juice and zest. Sprinkle with some fresh parsley or cilantro/coriander when cooked. Top with breadcrumbs and butter if you wish.

Use panko breadcrumbs instead of breadcrumbs. Use fresh chillies instead of ground pepper for this option.

Add fresh red chillies, de-seeded and cut lengthways and 1 teaspoon of Ras El Hanout (a complex Moroccan spice) or use ½ teaspoon of Harissa (see recipe page 59). Sprinkle with some fresh parsley, mint or cilantro/coriander when cooked. Top with breadcrumbs and butter if you wish. Note: Make your own Ras El Hanout with any of the following spices (always best if you grind them yourself): cardamom, nutmeg, allspice, cinnamon, chillies, cloves and fennel and numerous other flavours, such as lavender and rose buds.

6 scallops, cleaned but left in their shells

1 pinch salt and freshly ground pepper

1 garlic clove, finely chopped or 2 scallions/spring onions, finely chopped and sautéed in a little oil or butter

1 tablespoon finely chopped flat-leaf parsley

1 tablespoon lemon juice and grated lemon zest

3 tablespoons breadcrumbs made from 1–2-day-old bread mixed with 1 tablespoon of extra virgin olive oil or butter

*Paprika is called pimenton in Spain. It has a smoky taste, but if you do not have it in your spice rack use common paprika instead. I sometimes like to add cooked cannellini beans to this.*

# Cockles with Spanish Flavours

*Serves 6*

extra virgin olive oil, for frying

2 onions, thinly sliced

1 teaspoon pimenton (sweet)

½ teaspoon pimenton (hot)

2 cloves garlic, minced

4 medium ripe tomatoes, peeled and chopped (or tinned)

½ cup white wine (or Manzanilla or Fino sherry)

36 oz/1 kg cockles (they are usually sold cleaned)

2 tablespoon finely chopped parsley

10½–14 oz/300–400 g canned cannellini beans (optional)

Heat some extra virgin olive oil in a frying pan and sauté the onions on low heat till they soften; add the pimenton and garlic, stir gently for 1 minute.

Add the tomatoes and wine or sherry, cover and simmer until the sauce has thickened.

Add the cockles and parsley (and optional cannellini beans).

Cover and cook until they have opened, shaking the saucepan occasionally to distribute the heat evenly.

*These are simply cooked and garnished with a soffritto—a very common flavour base element in Italian cooking and very fragrant, usually containing olive oil and herbs. Mussels can be cooked the same way. You will need two saucepans, one for the cockles and one for the soffritto.*

*Mussels and vongole release their juices and seawater and so I never add salt when I am cooking these.*

# Vongole with soffritto

### Serves 6

**SOFFRITTO**
½ cup extra virgin olive oil
4 cloves garlic, finely chopped
1 small bunch of flat-leaf parsley

½ cup white wine
36 oz/1 kg vongole (also called pipis, clams or cockles)—they are usually sold cleaned

To make the soffritto, heat the olive oil in a wide pan, add the garlic and parsley and sauté on high heat—it should sizzle and the parsley should turn bright green.

To prepare the cockles, place wine in a large saucepan, add the cockles, cover and simmer until they have opened.

Shake the saucepan occasionally to distribute the heat evenly.

When they have opened, add the soffritto and serve.

Present the cockles with fresh bread to mop up the juices.

*I always refused cooked oysters until I was introduced to them ages ago. I was given a choice: you could eat them with a black bean topping or with a dressing of scallion/spring onion and ginger. Now, years later, those optional dressings are common and many others have been added besides. It is a very simple process and the oysters are warmed rather than cooked.*

# Baked oysters with ginger and scallions

## Serves 6

Place the oysters on a baking sheet/tray.

Place the ginger on top of the oysters; add a drop of soy onto each and grill (under top element in an oven) for 1 minute.

Top with the spring onion, criss-crossed over the oysters.

Heat the oil and sesame oil until it is very hot and splash it over the top of the oysters.

Serve immediately.

Your guests may also like Oyster Shooters (see page 142).

18 fresh oysters, opened

1 tablespoon fresh ginger, grated or thinly cut in julienne strips

1 tablespoon soy sauce

scallions/spring onions, cut into very thin strips 1¾–2 in/4–5 cm long (calculate 2–4 strips per oyster)

4 tablespoons vegetable oil mixed with 1 teaspoon sesame seed oil

*My favourite way to eat oysters is with a squeeze of lemon juice. I also like to eat cockles and mussels this way—I encourage you to try them raw sometime. But they must be fresh.*

*However, I know that some people like to eat oysters with sauces and if I have guests I do make some separate sauces and put them either in small jugs with a spoon or in little bowls (if the sauce is too thick) so that those who wish to can help themselves.*

# Fresh oysters with a Japanese-inspired dressing

*Serves 6*

18 oysters, shucked

JAPANESE-INSPIRED DRESSING
1 tablespoon soy sauce
1 tablespooon mirin
1 tablespoon lemon juice
1 tablespoon fresh ginger, finely
   grated
1 tablespoon finely chopped
   cilantro/coriander
1 tablespoon chopped scallion/
   spring onion

Combine all the dressing ingredients together, and vary ingredients to suit your tastes.

Add the dressing to the oysters.

I also sometimes add a small squirt of wasabi to the dressing, but be careful, because not everybody likes to have their top palate blown off!

*Pieces of skewered fish or shellfish are easy to cook and present. We're familiar with satays and kebabs, maybe even brochettes. In Italy, they are called* spiedini *and in Turkey they are called* miye tava. *If you have eaten* miye tava, *the mussels are deep-fried in a batter and taste delicious. But I prefer to grill food rather than fry it, and so I am providing this alternative. The flavours of the marinade and the sauce are Middle Eastern. Use skewers if you wish or toothpicks. If you are using wooden skewers, soak them in water for 10 minutes beforehand so they don't catch fire on the barbecue. I also use white wine when I am steaming the mussels, but this is optional.*

# Mussel brochettes with Middle Eastern flavours

*Serves 6*

24 mussels, scrubbed, bearded
  (4 mussels per person)
½ cup water (or wine)

MARINADE
1 tablespoon za'atar
grated peel of 1 lemon
½ cup extra virgin olive oil

Wash, clean and de-beard mussels. Shake them to remove excess moisture. Place the mussels and water, or wine, in a large saucepan, cover and cook over high heat, shaking the pan occasionally. Cook them until their shells have slightly opened.

Drain, remove the mussels from shells, and place on kitchen paper to dry.

To make the marinade, use the Middle Eastern spice called za'atar or make up your own mixture using ground dried thyme, roasted sesame seeds, sumac, dried marjoram and dried oregano. Try a combination using 1 teaspoon of each and add a little salt.

Add the mussels to the marinade and leave for about 10 minutes.

Thread 2 to 4 mussels onto toothpicks or skewers and grill on the barbecue for 1–3 minutes. Turn once.

Serve with either Walnut Sauce or you may choose a Sicilian Pesto (recipes on page 180).

*In the Middle East and Turkey miye tava are traditionally presented with this walnut sauce. I have seen alternative recipes where tahini is added instead, or ground almonds, or a mixture of ground almonds and pistachio. This thick sauce is traditionally made with a mortar and pestle, but a food processor can also be used.*

## Walnut Sauce (Tarator)

2 slices of white bread
(sourdough is best)
½ cup walnuts
1–2 cloves garlic, mashed
salt
½ cup extra virgin olive oil
lemon juice or a little yoghurt
(optional)
½ cup fresh basil leaves or
fresh marjoram (optional)

Remove the crusts from the bread, soak briefly in water and squeeze dry.

Grind the walnuts in a food processor until finely ground. Add 1–2 cloves of mashed garlic, salt and the squeezed bread.

Slowly add the oil, more if it's needed. The mixture should be thick and creamy. When served it may need to be stirred from time to time as some of the oil may separate.

I find that a little sharpness enhances the sauce. If you like, add a little lemon juice or some yoghurt. This also thins the paste. If you like, add ½ cup fresh basil leaves or fresh marjoram, but this is not a common practice.

*This traditional Sicilian pesto is also good with the mussel brochettes. There are many names and variations to this recipe (the most common names written in Italian are Pesto Trapanese or Matarocco) but this is my favourite combination and it is from Trapani, once settled by Arabs.*

## Mataroccu (Sicillian pesto)

8–10 cloves garlic
14 oz/400 g fresh ripe tomatoes,
peeled, seeded and chopped
1 cup almonds or pine nuts
1½ cup basil leaves, finely sliced
½ cup parsley, finely chopped
1 cup extra virgin olive oil (your
most fragrant) or as much as
the pesto absorbs
salt and red pepper flakes to
taste

This pesto is best prepared using a mortar and pestle. Pound the garlic in the mortar with a little salt to make a paste. Add some of the tomato, nuts, some herbs and a little oil, and pound some more.

Keep on adding a few ingredients at a time, until they have all been used up and you have a homogenous, smooth sauce.

If using a food processor, first grind the nuts. Add the rest of the ingredients and process until creamy. Add the finely chopped herbs last of all and pulse them for a very short time to prevent the grassy taste that a food processor tends to produce. Canned tomatoes are not appropriate.

*A friend sent me this recipe and I am going to include it just how she sent it.*
*I love the way that she has written it. It is exactly how we speak, how we used to write recipes and how I like to*
*cook. It also reminds me of how my Italian relatives cook, a little bit of this, a little bit of that, nothing is ever*
*measured precisely. The recipe continues to evolve and is likely to change next time depending of what she has in*
*her cupboard or is growing in her garden (she has a massive herb and vegetable garden).*

# Mussels with a cilantro and peanut pesto

Asian-type pestos are fairly generic and mine leaves out palm sugar and fish sauce and substitutes peanut oil with grapeseed oil but, once again, as I have all the leaves and herbs in the garden, I make this quite often.

Mine is just a couple of handfuls of cilantro/coriander, 6–8 cloves of garlic, a couple of handfuls of raw shelled peanuts, some Thai basil leaves, grapeseed oil, a small green chilli or two depending on how hot, a large lime and a chunk of ginger for extra heat and tang although sometimes I use galangal if have it instead.

This is all whizzed in a blender until smooth and I add extra lime or oil if it is too solid.

To make the mussels, I just add a few tablespoons of the pesto to the smoking grapeseed oil in a wok, give the pesto a very quick stir so it doesn't start to darken too much. I throw in the mussels, let the juice run out of the shells and serve when they are all open, in about 5 minutes.

This combination is also good if you use cockles.

couple of handfuls cilantro/
   coriander
6–8 cloves garlic
couple of handfuls raw shelled
   peanuts
Thai basil leaves
grapeseed oil
1–2 small green chillies, to taste
1 large lime
a chunk of ginger or galangal
about 36 oz/1 kg mussels,
   cleaned and de-bearded

*These little morsels are very popular, but I think that this is because some people just cannot resist the taste of bacon. I was asked to bring these to a function recently and replaced the bacon with prosciutto. The choice is yours. Serve these bites with toothpicks (soaked in water for 10 minutes beforehand) or use small metal skewers. Some people remove the coral from the scallop. I never do.*

# Scallops wrapped in prosciutto with a fennel salad

## Serves 6

Preheat the oven to 350°F/180°C.

Pat the scallops dry on kitchen paper.

Mix together the chilli flakes, salt and cumin or fennel. Lay out the strips of prosciutto and sprinkle with the spice mix.

Wrap the strip of prosciutto around each scallop.

Thread the scallops onto toothpicks and ensure that the prosciutto is secured to the scallop.

Place on a prepared baking sheet/tray lined with baking parchment/paper. If you feel that the prosciutto is not very fatty you may wish to lightly oil the paper (or use butter) before placing the scallops on to it.

Bake for about 5–6 minutes, turning only once.

They are ready when the prosciutto is crisp.

If you wish, you could make a small salad of very thinly sliced fennel dressed simply with extra virgin olive oil, wine vinegar, salt and pepper. Thinly sliced oranges also go well with fennel.

18 large scallops (or you could use shelled green shrimp/ prawns or fresh mussels)

¼ teaspoon chilli flakes

pinch of salt

½ teaspoon cumin mixed together or use ground fennel seeds for a totally different flavour

6 slices prosciutto, sliced very thinly, cut into 12 long strips

Minced fish

*I've found that fresh raw crabmeat sticks together quite well without having to use any binding ingredients. If you are using frozen crabmeat, make sure that it is well drained and add egg white. I do not think that canned crab is suitable for this recipe. These crab balls are easy to eat and full of fresh crab flavour. They can be served hot or cold.*

# Crab balls

### Makes about 18 balls

14 oz/400 g fresh crabmeat
salt and pepper to taste
egg white, lightly beaten
    (optional)
salt and pepper, to taste
all-purpose/plain flour, enough
    to lightly coat the balls
1–2 eggs, lightly beaten
breadcrumbs, enough to lightly
    coat the balls
oil to deep-fry

The crabmeat is easier to remove from the crabs if they have been in the freezer for a short time, but not frozen. Shred the crabmeat with a fork, add seasoning and with your fingers make small balls, the size of golf balls and put them in the fridge. These can be made several hours beforehand.

If you're worried about them falling apart, you can mix in some egg white before forming the balls.

Dip the balls in flour or dip them in flour, beaten egg and breadcrumbs before deep-frying. Remove them from the oil once they are lightly golden.

They are delicious eaten unaccompanied, but they can also be presented with a dipping sauce. For dipping sauces, see recipe for Fried Shrimp Balls with Dipping Sauces on page 189.

*These shrimp/prawn balls are really versatile and convenient. One of my friends presents them as a starter or in a broth with noodles with fresh Asian herbs and flavourings. This mixture can also be used to fill wonton wrappers, then steamed, poached or deep-fried. The shrimp/prawn balls can be prepared the day before and cooked just before serving or cooked earlier and served at room temperature. All can be presented and served with a dipping sauce.*

# Fried shrimp balls with dipping sauces

## Makes 16 balls

Pat dry the shrimp with paper towel. Chop them into into small pieces or briefly pulse them in a food processor (the texture should not be smooth) and place in a bowl. Add all the other ingredients, except the peanut oil, and combine well.

Shape the mixture into bite-sized balls and place on a lined plate or tray. Refrigerate, covered, until required.

Heat 2–3 tablespoons of peanut oil in a frying pan over medium heat. When hot, add half of the shrimp balls and fry, turning them until golden and cooked through. It should take about 3–4 minutes.

Place on a plate lined with paper towel to soak up any excess oil. Cover with a piece of foil. Add more oil to the pan, heat and then cook the remaining shrimp balls.

Place cooked balls onto a platter and garnish with fresh cilantro/coriander leaves. Serve with a dipping sauce.

10½ oz/300 g uncooked shrimp/ prawns, shelled and deveined
1 tablespoon ginger, grated
1 clove garlic, finely chopped
3 cilantro/coriander roots, finely chopped
1 scallion/spring onion, finely sliced
1 teaspoon oyster sauce
½ teaspoon sesame oil
1 egg yolk
1/3 cup soft breadcrumbs
peanut or vegetable oil, for frying
cilantor/coriander leaves, to garnish

DIPPING SAUCE 1 • 2 tablespoons light soy sauce • 1 tablespoon dry sherry or white wine • 1 tablespoon water • 1 teaspoon sugar 2 teaspoons ginger, grated • a few drops of sesame oil  a few drops of chilli oil (optional)

DIPPING SAUCE 2 • 3 tablespoons fish sauce • 2 tablespoons rice vinegar • 2 tablespoons lime juice • 1 tablespoon sugar • 2 tablespoons water • red chilli, finely shredded

In separate bowls, combine the dressing ingredients. Taste and adjust the seasoning. Pour into shallow serving bowls to serve.

*Polpette is the Italian word for meatballs. You can use any type of fish—no bones, no skin. My favourites are made with sardines and for this version the skin is left on.*

*They come in their own sauce. They have Sicilian flavours and are poached in a tomato salsa. If you prefer them fried, shallow fry them in a little extra virgin olive oil and serve them plain with a squeeze of lemon.*

*You may think that the ingredients could also be Middle Eastern and this is not surprising when you look at Sicily's history.*

# Fish balls in a tomato salsa

## Polpette di pesce
### *Makes about 18 balls*

17½ oz/500 g fish
½ cup pecorino cheese, grated
½ cup currants
½ cup pine nuts
½ cup finely chopped parsley or
    fresh mint
½ teaspoon lemon zest
½ teaspoon ground cinnamon
2 cloves garlic, minced
salt and a few chilli flakes
1 egg
1 cup fresh breadcrumbs

TOMATO SALSA
½ cup extra virgin olive oil
clove of garlic
a little salt
17½ oz/500 g red tomatoes,
    peeled and chopped (or
    canned or passata)

Cut the fish into chunks and mince using a meat grinder or food processor.

Combine all of the ingredients (except those for the salsa)—the mixture should be quite firm and hold its shape. Shape into 18 balls.

To make the tomato salsa, in a saucepan, large enough to hold the polpette, heat the olive oil, add the garlic, a little salt and the tomatoes.

Bring the mixture to the boil then lower the heat and reduce to thicken slightly for about 5 minutes.

Add the polpette, cover and braise for 8–10 minutes.

Serve hot. And pass around some bread to mop up the juices.

For a variation, use other Mediterranean flavours: preserved lemon peel instead of grated lemon, fresh cilantro/coriander instead of parsley, omit the cheese, add cumin.

*Zucchini/courgette fritters are found throughout the Middle East, southern Italy and Greece. They are called keftedes in Greece. They are just so simple to make and you can alter the taste by using different herbs or sauces. I do make them plain, but marinated white anchovies or uncooked whitebait can easily be added to the mixture. You could also present the keftedes plain, accompanied with white, marinated anchovies (boquerones). The combination goes well together. For an Italian version (frittele di zucchine), replace the feta with 2½ oz/80 g of grated parmesan cheese or pecorino cheese and use oregano or wild fennel instead of the dill.*

# Zucchini and mint fritters with marinated white anchovies
## Keftedes
### Serves 6

24 oz/700 g medium zucchini/ courgette, shredded

1 teaspoon salt

1 tablespoon extra virgin olive oil

2 eggs

4 oz/100 g crumbled feta

1 cup fresh mint and parsley, or dill and parsley, finely chopped

2½ oz/80 g all-purpose/plain flour

2 scallions/spring onions, finely chopped

freshly ground black pepper

extra virgin olive oil, for frying

1–2 tablespoons uncooked whitebait (dipped in flour) or marinated white anchovies (drained)


## MARINATED WHITE ANCHOVIES

36 fl oz/1 kg commercially marinated white anchovies

4 cloves garlic, finely chopped

1 cup parsley, finely chopped

3 scallions/spring onions

extra virgin olive oil, to cover

Grate the zucchini, add about 1 teaspoon of salt and leave to drain in a colander for at least 30 minutes. Squeeze it to extract excess water.

Combine the zucchini and the olive oil with the eggs. Fold in all of the other ingredients and some black pepper. The mixture should resemble a smooth thick batter.

Place heaped tablespoons of courgette batter in the hot oil; allow room for the fritters to spread and to fry. Flatten them with a spatula if necessary and fry them until they are golden. Drain on paper towels and serve.

Alternatively, you can also bake them. Place small heaps on a baking sheet/tray covered with oiled baking parchment/ paper and bake at 430°F/220°C for 10–15 minutes.

Serve them with white anchovies on the side and fresh bread.

## MARINATED WHITE ANCHOVIES

Drain the anchovies, add the garlic, parsley and the onions, and cover them with extra virgin olive oil.

Leave them to marinate for at least one day. After that they will be superb. In two days time, they will taste even better. White anchovies are not salty like typical anchovies and they are great in salads, on pizzas, incanapés and on top of crusty bread.

# Fish sliders

During my most recent trip to Italy I was amazed to see how many hip bars specialise in making burgers. They are considered a fashionable snack to accompany wine or beer.

Burgers, like pizza are now universal and have been miniaturised and these mini burgers are known as sliders.

Sliders are perfect food for when you're entertaining—they are an easy size to hold and so easy to slide into your mouth.

# Sliders made with crab cakes

*Makes 10*

Process the fish until smooth. Add the crabmeat but don't process too much.

Transfer to a bowl and add the mayonnaise and half of the breadcrumbs, pus any other flavourings and seaonings you wish, but not too much or you'll lose the taste of the fish.

Divide the mixture up into balls that will fit the size of your mini burger buns, toss in the breadcrumbs then flatten and refrigerate until needed.

Heat some oil in a shallow frying pan until very hot. Shallow-fry the patties until golden on both sides, place on kitchen paper then place on a baking sheet/tray in 350°F/180°C oven for about 15 minutes.

Serve the patties on mini burger buns with a little dollop of chilli sauce. Eat the patties hot or cold.

4½ oz/125 g white fish

17½ oz/500 g raw crabmeat (if frozen, drain it well)

1 tablespoon egg mayonnaise

10½ oz/300 g fresh breadcrumbs (made with 1–2-day-old bread)

½ teaspoon Tabasco, optional

1 teaspoon Worcestershire sauce, optional

6 scallions/spring onions, chopped, optional

oil, for frying

10 small burger buns or bread rolls, available from bakeries and supermarkets

chilli sauce, to serve

*If you prefer to present them warm, the patties can also be warmed either in an oven or a microwave before you place them into small hot rolls, warmed in an oven beforehand. For the burgers presented at room temperature, you can add soft green salad leaves in the roll (young arugula/rocket leaves or cress or very finely sliced lettuce).*

# Fish sliders with fresh herb paste

*Makes 6*

Cut the fish into chunks and mince using a meat grinder or food processor—I do not like the mixture to be too fine.

Combine all of the ingredients except the oil—the mixture should be quite firm and hold its shape. You may need a few more breadcrumbs, depending on the type of fish you use. Shape into 6 balls and flatten them slightly.

Fry them in hot oil and drain them on some kitchen paper.

Stuff the patties into rolls and place a dollop of herb paste into them before serving. Hold the rolls together with a toothpick or a small metal skewer.

## HERB PASTE

A simple paste can be made with any of the following fresh herbs: coriander, basil, mint, tarragon or chervil. My preferred method is to chop the herbs finely and mix all of the ingredients by hand. Rather than using olive oil, you can use egg mayonnaise.

6 small rolls suitable for mini-burgers
17½ oz/500 g fish, salmon or a mixture, see above
1 tablespoon fresh parsley, finely chopped
1 clove garlic, minced
salt and pepper to taste
1 small egg
½ cup fresh bread breadcrumbs
extra virgin olive oil for frying

## HERB PASTE

1 cup finely chopped fresh herbs
zest of 1 lemon or the skin of 1 preserved lemon, finely chopped
½ cup lemon juice, freshly squeezed
½ cup extra virgin olive oil
3–4 cloves garlic, crushed
salt and freshly ground black pepper, to taste

# Potato and fish croquettes
## with a difference

I rarely remember eating plain potatoes with my parents. My mother always used potatoes as an ingredient. For example, she made gnocchi or layered thin slices of potatoes with ham and cheese, put broth in them and baked them.

If we had mashed potatoes they contained a lot of butter and milk. They were topped with breadcrumbs, more butter and then baked until they formed a golden crust. Mashed potatoes were also used for making croquettes. But, again, the croquettes always contained other flavourings. Being fried, there was always a flavoursome crust on the outside.

*My sister-in-law makes these as a light lunch or dinner with salad. Her mother before her made the same patties. Seeing her recipe reminded me that my mother also used to make potato croquettes. She added anchovies or ham to hers.*

# Tuna or salmon patties

### *Makes 18–20 balls*

Combine the fish with the mashed potato, salt and pepper and the parsley. Add some fresh breadcrumbs if the mixture is wet.

Take a dessertspoon size amount of the mixture and roll into balls. Refrigerate for about a half an hour to settle the mixture.

Dip the balls into the beaten egg and then into the cornflake crumbs.

Heat some oil in a frying pan and shallow fry the balls. Flatten them with a spatula and turn them when they are brown.

Serve with some lemon wedges or a tasty mayonnaise.

10½ oz/300 g canned tuna, salmon or pink salmon, drained (remove skin and bones)

24 oz/700 g potatoes, peeled, cooked and mashed

salt and freshly ground pepper

½ cup finely chopped parsley

2 eggs, lightly beaten

2–3 tablespoons cornflake crumbs to coat (crushed cornflakes)

oil, to fry

lemon wedges, to serve

1–2 tablespoons fresh breadcrumbs

Mayonnaise, to serve (see recipe page 91)

*The French call them croquettes, Italians know them as crocchette. No cornflakes in these.*
*To stop them becoming soggy, boil the potatoes whole and then peel them once they are cool.*
*Instead of the anchovies, you could also use 4 oz/100 g of smoked eel or other smoked fish.*

# Crocchette di patate

## Makes 6–8

24½ oz/700 g potatoes

2 eggs, lightly beaten

2 cloves garlic, minced

½ cup parsley, finely chopped

4 anchovies, cut into small
    pieces (or 4 oz/100 g flaked
    smoked eel)

salt and freshly ground pepper

a little all-purpose/plain flour
    or breadcrumbs to coat the
    crocchette

extra virgin olive oil for frying

Cook the potatoes until soft (boil or use a microwave). Peel when cool enough to handle and use a ricer or a Mouli grater (a hand-operated tool designed for grating or pureeing small quantities of food) to mash them. Let cool completely.

Add the eggs, garlic, parsley and seasoning and the fish last of all.

Shape the mixture into egg-shaped patties and, just before frying, roll them in a little flour.

Heat up the oil in a frying pan on a medium-high heat. Fry the patties until golden, only turning once. Set aside on kitchen paper until all of the patties are cooked.

*This shrimp/prawn recipe is an old faithful from the 1970s. It came originally from a friend's mother-in-law. The recipe is really simple and it is also interesting to see how béchamel was used to bind the ingredients rather than the egg white used in the Asian fish balls, or the fresh bread and eggs in Mediterranean dishes that have replaced this type of cuisine. The recipe reminds me of Croquetas de jamón (ham croquettes or balls) or the Croquetas de bacalao that some Spaniards make with béchamel rather than potato. It's the same process and ingredients, except for the ham.*

# Vintage shrimp balls with old-fashioned tartare sauce

## Makes 12 balls

Melt the butter in a pan. Add the cornstarch and blend thoroughly.

Add the milk and cook until thickened, stirring constantly. Add more milk if the white sauce is too thick. Season with salt and pepper.

Cool, then add finely chopped shrimp and form into small balls.

Roll and coat the balls in a little cornstarch, then in beaten egg and finally in the breadcrumbs. Shake off excess.

Fry in hot oil until golden. Serve hot or cold.

Update this recipe with an Asian-flavoured dipping sauce or use this old-fashioned tartare sauce, which would be much more in keeping with the times.

### OLD-FASHIONED TARTARE SAUCE

Mix these ingredients together by hand.

1 oz/30 g butter
1 tablespoon cornstarch/corn flour
1 cup milk (approx.)
salt and pepper, to taste
12–16 large shrimp/prawns, cooked, cleaned and chopped finely
1–2 tablespoons extra cornstarch
1 egg, beaten with a fork
fine dry breadcrumbs (to coat)
vegetable oil for frying

### OLD-FASHIONED TARTARE SAUCE

1 cup good mayonnaise
2 tablespoons small-diced pickles or cornichons or capers
salt and freshly ground black pepper
a little parsley, finely chopped (use fresh tarragon if you have it!)

A popular street food in Morocco made with potato is maakouda batata. As you would expect with the foods of Morocco, these are endowed with aromatic flavours. They do not usually contain fish but the combination works well. These little flattened croquettes are made even more tasty when coated with a mixture of crushed cumin seeds and cracked pepper before frying. This is optional but I consider it essential. For this recipe you can use any type of cooked leftover fish or if you'd like to poach some fish, see the recipe for Poached Fish on page 84.

# Potato croquettes from Morocco
## Maakouda batata
### Makes 6–8 patties

24¾ oz/700 g potatoes
1 small onion, finely chopped
3 cloves garlic, minced
2 eggs, beaten
½ cup finely chopped cilantro/ coriander leaves
1 tablespoon cumin powder
1 tablespoon butter, melted
1 cup cooked fish, flaked
salt and pepper, to taste
1 tablespoon crushed cumin seeds
1 tablespoon cracked pepper (optional) or a little all- purpose/plain flour to coat the croquettes
extra virgin olive oil, for frying

Boil the potatoes until soft and mash them as in the previous recipe. Peel when they are cool enough to handle and use a ricer or a Mouli grater to mash.

Sauté the onion gently over low heat until soft and golden. Add the garlic and remove the pan from the heat. Let cool.

Mix in the eggs, cilantro, cumin powder, butter, fish, the onion and garlic mixture and seasoning.

Shape the potato mixture into small balls and then slightly flatten them (like patties).

Mix some crushed cumin seeds and pepper together and use this to coat the patties, or coat with a little flour if you prefer. Press the patties into the crushed mixture with your fingers.

Fry the patties in hot oil until golden. Serve hot.

Salt cod fritters can be found all over the Mediterranean and they have been introduced to other shores where Spanish or Italian peoples have settled. The cod can usually be bought from Italian or Spanish specialty stores. You need to begin preparations for this three days before because the salt cod will need to soak. Some salt cod is pre-soaked beforehand, so it is best to ask about this when you buy it. The fritters can be made with breadcrumbs or mashed potatoes. These are made with potatoes. The French make Brandade and the Spaniards Croquetas de bacalao. The Italians make Polpette di baccalà.

Because I like the taste of salt cod, I make these fritters fairly plain and then serve them with a tasty sauce. Eat them hot or cold.

# Salt cod fritters with green olive paste or saffron mayonnaise

### *Makes about 6 balls*

9 oz/250 g salt cod fillets (also sold as baccala or bacalao)
1 bay leaf
10½ oz/300 g floury potatoes
2 small eggs, lightly beaten
½ cup parsley, finely chopped
a little all-purpose/plain flour
extra virgin olive oil, for frying

First, soak the fish to remove the salt: first rinse any excess salt off the cod, then put it into a large bowl and cover with cold water.

Leave to soak in the fridge for 36–48 hours, changing the water three to four times a day.

Once it's been soaked, put the salt cod into a pan with the bay leaf and cover with fresh cold water and bring to the boil over a medium heat.

Remove the pan from the heat and leave in the water to stand to cool. When the fish has cooled, remove the skin and any bones and flake the flesh with a fork.

Cook the potatoes whole until soft (boil or use a microwave). Peel when cool enough to handle and use a ricer or a mouli grater to mash them. Let cool completely.

Add the potatoes, eggs and parsley to the flaked cod.

Shape the mixture into small balls and put them in the fridge for 30 minutes or so to firm them up.

Next, roll the cod balls in four and fry in hot extra virgin olive oil until golden, about 3–4 minutes.

Serve with a dollop of either green olive paste or saffron mayonnaise.

## GREEN OLIVE PASTE

Combine all of the paste ingredients (except for the parsley or mint and seasoning) in a small food processor. Add the herbs and seasoning and mix gently by hand.

## SAFFRON MAYONNAISE

Mix the egg with a little salt in the blender or food processor, or in a clean jar (if using a stick blender).

Slowly add the extra virgin olive oil in a thin, steady stream through the feed tube while the blender or processor is running.

Before adding additional oil, ensure that the oil that has already been added has been incorporated completely.

Add a tablespoon of fresh lemon juice when the mayonnaise is creamy.

Gently mix in the saffron and water.

### GREEN OLIVE PASTE
¼ cup extra virgin olive oil
1 cup pitted green olives
2 tablespoons drained capers
1 garlic clove, minced
1 teaspoon lemon juice
½ cup chopped parsley or mint
(or a mixture of the two)
salt and freshly ground pepper,
to taste

### SAFFRON MAYONNAISE
1 egg
1–1½ cups extra virgin olive oil
1 tablespoon lemon juice
pinch of saffron, pre-softened in
a very little warm water

# About the author

Marisa Raniolo Wilkins is a lively fusion of cultures and experience. She was born to Sicilian parents in Ragusa, but she spent her childhood in the far northeast of Italy in the renowned port city of Trieste, where her parents met. Her mother's family had moved there in the 1930s and her father was posted there during the war. Trieste became their home until the family moved away.

Every summer, Marisa and her parents would pack up and travel the length of Italy from Trieste to Sicily to visit relatives in that exotic island. From an early age, she developed a fascination with the food and cooking of her Sicilian relatives and those who were living in Trieste.

In Marisa's family, quality produce and good cooking have always been highly valued. They put a premium on seasonal ingredients sourced locally. Marisa carries on that tradition and takes enormous pleasure in experiencing good food and sharing it with others. She spares no effort in preparing and serving exceptional food, knowing that it makes her and her guests feel good.

Over the years, Marisa has travelled many times to different parts of Italy, both for the joy of discovery and to visit her extended family. Every visit adds to her store of first-hand experience. In her travels to many other parts of the world, she has been inspired by culinary traditions and cultivation and preparation of local specialties.

Marisa's first book, *Sicilian Seafood Cooking*, was a comprehensive account of Sicilian cuisine and culture. It was also a way to document some of the classic, localised Sicilian dishes cooked by her family and what she has experienced in Sicily. It was published by New Holland in November 2011.

*Small Fishy Bites* is her second book. It celebrates the diversity and versatility of seafood and recognises the popularity of serving small helpings—easy, casual and varied dishes. It also reflects food that she has encountered in her travels in the Mediterranean countries and Asia and the food she shares with her friends.